WWW.SHERIKADUNCAN.COM

Sherika Duncan Enterprise, Inc. published books may be purchased for educational, business or sales promotional use. For information, please email the Sales Department at sales@sherikaduncan.com.

First Edition Printed, February 2022

Library of Congress Cataloging-in-Publication Data has been applied for.

ISBN: 978-1-7364355-8-8

IF I KNEW WHAT I KNOW NOW

Volume I

Foreword & Dedication

To the reader of this book series, it will be a deep dive into the lives of various characters who entertain the street life of crime, drugs, sex, murder, and violence. The intended language will remain purest throughout this book to convey the many volatile environments. This true story depicts several occurrences of drug trafficking, numerous sexual encounters, street violence, and a ton of wrong decisions captivated around musicality, street recognition, financial gain, independence, and respect.

A special thank you to Denise Lindsey & Rev. Kaite Lindsey for being there for me & giving me insight through my trials and tribulations. A very special thank you to the Back Cover model: Alveeta Wilson and to Sherika Duncan for bringing the book to life.

Table of Content

Chapter 1

"Studio Time"

"Man, stop bullshitting' Boss! Get this shit right, so we can get out of here!" Cancer also known as K.P. told Charles as he was in the booth, the place where he called his office. Cancer was on the ones and twos. He again set the beat in motion for his cousin to finish his verse.

"Just hit the record, fool! I got this!" snaps Charles. Some called him Boss, but those close to him call him C-Lo.

"Okay! On three! One, two," Cancer replied as he pointed.

"Yea, I'm ridin', I'm blazin', gotta get it, you haters be fakin'

They say I'm bent back fa all these pills I be takin'

Red, blue, plus I'm on dis good drank

Before I go broke, I'll mask up and take a bank

So serious bout dis money, what the fuck you niggas think

Pounds of dro-, rainbow colors of dis dank-"

C-Lo had come across fifty thousand dollars when his grandmother Rev. Katie passed away. She always inspired him to live out his dreams and let no one stop him. So, he put together the best studio that Tampa, Florida had ever seen, with live drums, live guitars, and pro equipment. He was an up-and-coming local rapper with dreams of making it big, so he wouldn't have to drive trucks for the rest of his life. He was working his way from the bottom to make it to the top. Blood, sweat, and tears. No help from his ex-friend, Phats.

Phats was the producer/rapper and CEO of BeastMode Records Inc. They fell out over something minor; C-Lo had more control over Phats' equipment than he did, and it was obvious C-Lo was a much better rapper and producer. You could feel the jealousy and envy in his heart grow every time they came together in the studio to make music. Let's just say C-Lo was the Boss and Phats wasn't. That was enough for Phats to get his equipment and take off. Now it was far from a problem because C-Lo had his own. Blood Money Entertainment. BME!

"Finished!" Cancer was done with the finishing touches and played back the song. "The hood gone love this one, Boss!" He blew out a slight laugh. "You outdid yourself with this one." Cancer finished mixing as he replayed the song. "Let's Flex! You ready?" Cancer asked.

"Yea. Let me run in the house and grab my shit!" C-Lo yelled over the music running from the garage where his studio was to his bedroom upstairs.

When he got there, he grabbed his Gucci bag, his Glock 17, and put it in his waistline. He ran back downstairs and jumped in the passenger seat of his new candy apple red super duty F-350 king ranch, ready for whatever.

***

"First Quarter"

Cancer pulled off, heading to the Rose Park Projects to pick up a package from his ace Sam-Bam, and a few others. He also had to go meet up with Meatball, Fish's brother, and Rex. The BMC Boyz had different spots on lock but were trying to set up shop in some old apartments for the whole BMC, aka the Byrd Money Clique. They had to count this money way before they had to get ready for the club.

Now Bam-Bam, also known as B.A.M., earned his name from being a *Bad Ass Motherfucker*. As a star running back for Hillsborough High, he was destined to be great. He'd take off dancing in the backfield, looking every bit of Marshawn Lynch, with his dreads hanging out his helmet trailing in the wind. I do mean a *Bad Ass Motherfucker*.

As they shot cross-town and turned off M.L.K. drive, Cancer flushed the gas to the floor showing off the high-powered V-8 engine. He was speeding down Central, blasting one of the joints C-Lo features on that was on his little brother's album *Grindin' Season*. He had some of the baddest, I mean prettiest and loudest, whips in the city. His super duty F-350 king ranch had four horns underneath it: two in the front bumper and two in the back bumper. It also had four twelves, four tens, and a handful of 8" kickers everywhere. You could hear it from blocks away.

As Cancer circled around Rose Park, you could see Bam and their boy Nut outside talking to two sexy chicks. When they crossed over Lake, the first person you saw was MeMe in his wheelchair. Standing next to him were Mario, Jit-Redd, Tree, and a host of others throughout the jets serving.

"Boss!" Bam hollered, throwing his hands up as he was smacking the big booty redbone chick across the backside. "What it do, Lo?"

He smirked as he approached the passenger's side. C-Lo replied, "I can't tell." As he paused and looked over at his boy, "What's popping Nut?" Nut threw up a pound, acknowledging him as he was talking to the other dark skin chicken head.

"I see what y'all boyz got going on, making it do what it do." C-Lo said.

"Man, ain't nothing," Nut replied. "Ain't nobody thinking about them hood rat hoes! I'm outcha grinding, getting dis pay up. What it is, is Tiger and Cowboy always chasing and hounding a brother, trying to find something on a nigga! You feel me!"

Lil Wayne: "The block is hot... The block is hot, hot, hot."

"Have anybody went in?" C-Lo asked Bam.

"Naw. You taught us better than that to be out here slipping! Ya Heard!" Nut yelled.

"Yea, I hear ya... You got that for me?" C-Lo asked.

"Definitely!" Bam turned and whistled. Jit-Redd went into their trap house and came back out with a package in hand within seconds. Bam handed it to C-Lo.

Without opening it, C-Lo asked, "45?"

"Hell yeah... I told you that he was gone cash check!" C-Lo cracked the Gucci bag; it was full of money. C-Lo broke a smile and replaced it with another Gucci off the back floor then handed it to Bam. "This Two?" Bam asked confused.

4

"Yeah bro, with two on consignment. You can handle that?" C-Lo replied.

"Definitely!"

"Okay, that's what it is, then. Get with me when she's done."

C-Lo had just got to brick status. He had been in the game on and off for years, but he really had come up from that money the night he shot and killed Lindsey's sister Dazaray.

***

"B.M.C."

Eric (Brown) McCloud, aka Big E, was selling C-Lo work way before he started messing with Mexico; he put the first brick in his hands. Ever since then, he'd been throwing up B.M.C. strong. Big E was, and still is, hard to catch up with. He's a smooth D-boy, one you wouldn't ever want to see, and had schooled C-Lo on his game. C-Lo was now trying to arrange for Bam his young BMClique the same exact setup.

"Bet that up! Oh, I almost forgot! I talked to my main man Capone for you," Bam said.

"Oh, true that? Wat buddy talking bout?" C-Lo asked.

Bam emphasized, "He just doing his thing! I told him you wanted to get with him."

C-Lo replied, "For show. What he say?"

Bam answered, "He told me to drop you the digits, so you could reach out and bark at 'em!"

Capone's, and Bam's so-called best friend had the areas: Rosa Park, Rearview Terrace, and Central Park. He was from a small island in the West Indies, better known as Trinidad and

Tobago. He'd been in the States for only five or six years, fresh out of high school. In those few years, he had already built up a mini empire.

C-Lo and the BMClique consisted of C.J. (R.I.P.), Meats, Main, Jit-Redd, Nut, Meatball, Fish, Rex, T-Red, Dump, Big Yoda Boy, 5P, and a few other little homies that were getting money with him, and of course, Sam-Bam. They'd have the streets on lock if it wasn't for Capone.

Bam was his main hustler; he was basically Lieutenant of their little crew. Don't get me wrong, they were a team full of go-getters, but he was already doing his thing, pushing nice numbers without them. Even though he was making 40 to 50 thousand dollars a week by himself, he could have tripled that if Capone wasn't in the picture. C-Lo wasn't selfish, far from that. He felt there was enough dough in the city for them all to eat.

The BMC Boyz had a few spots on lock, but he didn't have College Hill, Ponce de Leon, nor a bunch of other highly populated dope holes that were the real money makers. C-Lo was moving in on Rosa Park but he needed to get Capone on his team, or at least get him too re-up from him. With that, he'd clear over $250,000 a month easily, while he wouldn't have to do anything except lay on the couch playing his P3. He knew realistically, he didn't have enough territory to clear the numbers. Those BMC Boyz getting money!!!

The person C-Lo did have a problem with was Phats; he was just pure evil. The last time they were in the studio, their little homie Lil Vinny, aka Lil V, was with them.

Lil Wayne: "Jeah! Call 'em the ghost, Why, fuck 'em they can't see him/ Married to this life, I do! Fa getting mo money they gone need him/ Cause I eat MC's, cereals name 50's.../(Ha!) I talk plenty,

*my shit smell like money/ C-Lo told me, don't stop just get money!
/smoother than Weezy lady Cash Money be da pay me/ my pimp
game swagger, harder than hovie baby ...."*

The last thing Lil V told C-Lo was that he didn't trust Phats. Later that same evening, Lil V was found dead. Somebody had put two holes in his chest and one in his temple right after leaving the studio. The only thing C-Lo could remember from his gifted artist was his last words, "I don't trust that nigga Phats, watch 'em, Boss." C-Lo just knew Phats had something to do with his death, but he couldn't prove it.

The word on the streets was Phats was getting money on Cross Fletcher, and in the West, from selling the beans and that good dro. He was still in the studio pushing new artists but had them stuck making diss songs about C-Lo and his camp. B.J., the homeboy of 500 Proof -5P that is -, was still over at BeastMode Records but eventually saw Phats was a lousy businessman. 5P ended up moving to Orlando, Florida but still associated with B.M.E. on the music tip.

Nobody gave a damn about Phats or what Phats was doing because everybody was doing their own thing. Cancer was going to college, studying computer engineering. He was only around when C-Lo was around; making music, hitting the club, or when it was time to party. Some days he drove for him if not Jit-Redd, and they'd go on what C-Lo calls his money route, like today.

After they went and picked up money from Fish, Main, Meats, and Meatball, they headed to Raven. She was an older chick that helped school C-Lo on the powder game when he sold nothing but green. Apple Bottom was her nickname, but he called her by her real name, Raven, especially when they had sex. She kept most of his drug money in a wall safely stashed in the brick fireplace he installed in her home.

They also stopped at his two cooks, Big Yoda Boy and Snapp', hideout. Snapp had his own label as well called 4-E-B, also known as 4-Ever Ballin Records. They both cooked up and bagged ounces, 1-2-5's, up to his quarter bricks, half bricks, and stamped his keys with their special B.M. bird.

O.J. Da Juice Man: "Quarter bricks, half bricks, whole bricks Aye!"

Chapter 2

"THE BEGINNING"

C-Lo and Cancer headed to Playboy's barbershop to get their haircut. Even though Cancer would kill a nigga for him, he never wanted any part of the dope game. He had never said anything about it to C-Lo, but God put it on his heart to say something. It was time to have that much needed talk. Before he could open his mouth, C-Lo called Capone.

"Hello!" 'What it do, blood?"

"Who the fuck is this?" Capone asked.

"Dis C-Lo fool."

"Oh. What it do, main man?" Capone said.

"You know wat it is. We need to get together so we can have a meeting of the minds," C-Lo said slowly.

"So, what it be bout?" Capone asked.

"What you mean, fool! Business wat else! How we gone eat nigga!" C-Lo yelled. They both paused.

"Man, not to sound rude main man. I'm good... The God already eating fam," said Capone.

"I'm just saying'! I'm talking bout on a whole different level than me or you not even on yet. You feel me?"

"Yeah, I feel ya... Well, run down the B-bout. Look. I don't drop lines over the waves first rule I learnt. This what it is though. Let's connect up at, let's say, in Ybor City at Full Moon. That way we can sit down, talk business, and have a drink," Capone replied.

"What time ya talking'?" C-Lo asked.

"Tonight! Around let's say... 9:30 or 10. My lady's dad is doing his promotion thing I'm trying to check out, so I'll be down there anyway," C-Lo replied.

"Bet that up," Capone replied.

"Be safe."

"Be safe fool," Capone replied before hanging up.

Meanwhile, Cancer was pulling up in the Playboys Barbershop parking lot. After he parked, he stared down at C-Lo.

"What's wrong, Blood?" C-Lo asked.

"Boss, you know I ain't on that blood shit, C," Cancer said.

"Whatever. Looks like something on ya mind!" C-Lo replied.

"I'm having some bad vibes for some reason. I think you should slow down a little bit, folks."

"K.P. You know I ain't on that folk shit, but I mean. I don't know why. Everything couldn't be better, cuzzo. Is it that nigga Capone?"

"Naw! Nothing like that, or out of the ordinary, but I feel something! You might just be moving super-fast, cuzzo. Bruh, you don't need for shit! You are the hood, my nigga, and you not wanting for shit. Now is your time, cuz. What you need to do is get deeper off in this music shit and start up some business. You said that was your dream... You used to say that! You trapped your ass off when we stay together in Temple Terrace to get to this point."

C-Lo's head dropped towards his lap as he continued to listen to K.P. "I remember! Like it was yesterday. We sat in our living room, and you told me you were gone get your weight up, make bout 100,000, then you were gone. You didn't have anything starting off with 40 Cuz! Remember that? Now you got a chance of a lifetime. I think you should take off and never look back."

"I know," C-Lo replied.

"I know you said that! What happens? You almost a millionaire cuz!" KP. shouted.

"I know K.P., but a million ain't no money! Ya, hear me! I got a half a dozen spots on lock, and if this deal goes down with this Mexican Santana dude, it won't be no need to even turn back."

"Boss, that's greed. I wouldn't be telling you this if I didn't have nothing but love for you, cuz," Cancer said.

"I feel ya. Let me do this, then I'm out fa good, straight up."

"Boss. I ain't joking... I'm not talking to be talking. I'm for real, C! Not to be in ya business or no shit, or to spook you up. I'm telling you what God loves and nothing but... Look! Niggas out here hating hard bruh. I can see it in their eyes, and I know you. Just don't wait until it's too late, Boss. I love you, bruh, but it's a lot of motherfuckers who want to see you fail, fam. People envy you! You can't trust nobody, C. Nobody. Remember that!"

Chapter 3

"BOUNCE DAT AZZ"

C-Lo and Cancer arrived at the hot club Sky in Ybor City. They were at the bar getting some drinks and bumped right into Tiffany's best friend, Coco. "You seen Tiff?" C-Lo yelled over the music that was blasting.

Lil John ft Ying Yang Twins: *"Get low! Get low! From the window – to the wall!"*

"She went somewhere with her dad!" Coco replied.

"What you said?" C-Lo asked.

"I said she stepped out with her dad!!!" Coco yelled before looking up at Cancer, "Hey K.P.!"

Cancer turned towards Rasheeda with a half-ass smile, "Hey Coco. What's good?"

"You! Why haven't you called me?" she said.

"Been in them books, you know how it is!" Cancer paused then said, "Well, maybe…maybe you don't!" He laughed and she couldn't help but giggle herself.

"You just a comedian na-ah!!! Oh, look! There goes Chief!" said Rasheeda.

Chief is C-Lo's little brother, three years younger than him. He was extremely confident in his own skin; a pretty boy with hella pretty boy swag. He always rocked the newest gear and was in his own lane. Being a very spiritual person, he was bright, knowledgeable, witty, headstrong, and always on his toes.

He and Cancer were running buddies, anytime Cancer wasn't with C-Lo he'd be with Chief. Chief had a thing for white girls and always kept the baddest one, like his baby mama, Tanya. They were both the same age. They'd attended Leto High, where they met and fell in love. Fresh out of high school, they had two kids back-to-back- Isaiah and Elijah - but that didn't stop him from doing his thing.

Chief also rapped a little bit; really, he was a beast when it came to the mic. With 5P at their side, they really should've been blown up. He kept plenty of money and hoes. He was a gifted student and had pursued his fine arts degree while managing a big company, mostly by himself. Chief was the one who really made B.M.E. Records official, with all of his executive connections.

He swagged up to everybody gliding, with his deep waves and his Steve Harvey tape line. He smiled, showing off his new golds and smoking the fattest backwood you have ever seen, with a fatter one tucked behind his ear. Why do you think they call him Chief!?

"What's good, bruh?" C-Lo said.

"I'll show you in a second," Chief responded, pulling on the wood before he handed it to him. "What's good, Cuzzo?"

13

"It looks like you got it, Pimpin! That good, that is. I see you shining! How much did they run ya?" Cancer asked.

"Bout two bands," Chief said with a smirk.

"Hey Chief," Coco yelled and waved, trying to speak over the new T.I. that was playing in the background.

T.I: *"Throw ya hands up high! Don't you want to kick it with a stand-up guy!"*

"Nothing," Chief replied. He brushed her off nonchalantly as he turned back to check out a group of four of the baddest females strolling by.

Everybody was drinking, enjoying themselves having a good ole time. Rex big balling ass so happened to be in the building, doing it big like them boyz from the Westside always did. Dump even came through with a couple of Drak Boyz from the Springs, showing off a Drak tattoo he'd re-drawn of a skull dripping with blood that had a dagger going through the top. All the boys started showing off their new tattoos when C-Lo looked over at Tiffany. She was staring off with an annoyed look on her face, C-Lo looked over to see what she was looking at and it was her dad approaching the bar where they were all gathered.

"What's going on? Fellows? Ladies?" Tiffany's dad, Gee, short for Gator, said.

Everybody responded to him in unison, "Nothing Gee!"

"What it do, old man?" C-Lo greeted him.

"Couldn't be better. I hope y'all enjoying your time. If you all need drinks, feel free to tell the lady bartender right there, and she'll give y'all whatever. It's on me," Gator replied.

C-Lo wasn't having that. "No, it's on me!"

14

Tiffany walked straight over to C-Lo as he sat his drink down and melted straight into his arms after he embraced her. He pulled her closer, feeling his manhood rise down his leg. He cuffed his hands around her thin waist, then worked them around her huge phat bubble butt. Tiffany Tillman was her full name and everything about her was mesmerizing. Her skin was flawless, smoother than dark chocolate-covered kisses. Looking at her, you'd swear she'd taste like one too. She was three years younger than C-Lo and was his same height with heels on. She had stripper-type legs and a forty something inch booty to complement them. She had every curve of Buffie da Body with 38C's. Most people would often tell her she resembled the rapper Foxxy Brown or Kelly Rowland, but a sexier modeling type.

Tiffany was from Jacksonville, Florida and moved to Tampa five years ago, following her sister and dad. She had managed a fast-food restaurant for several years. But after an accident, she didn't work anymore. She just took care of her man as much as he took care of her.

C-Lo and Gee eased off to the side, "What's the business, old man?" C-Lo asked.

"That's enough of that old man stuff," Gator replied.

"Hahaha... My bad, pops!" C-Lo laughed.

"And don't call me pops, please! That makes me feel like I'm old for real."

"My bad, Gee. Oh yea, here's my last demo! I'm working on some new material right now as we speak, but it's a club jumper on that piece, track #2. It's called *Bounce Dat Azz*! Give it to D.J. Yayo for me! Tell 'em bump that joint for me."

"Will do, but I've been trying to open my own club in Dade City on Hwy 301, and my money is kind of funny right now. Feel me! That's what I wanted to talk to you about," Gator said. C-Lo listened as he continued to drink on his Remy with a splash of coke. "I need you to help me. Invest in it with me! Like, let's become partners! Go half with me so we can start this thang up! What do you say?"

C-Lo paused for a great while before responding, "Look ya hear me, my money kind of young right now. My dough ain't near bout right, Gee. I'm tied up in these two little projects I got in motion. Look, though, ya hear me. Let me power up like Mario's brothers, and when I can touch something, it's whatever! Plus, whenever I get into something especially like that, I got to keep it 100, whole undivided attention. Ya heard?"

"Yeah, okay, I can dig that. Just let me know ASAP. I got some people that know some people. They only want fifty bands down to buy it. We can have it up and jumping in no time. Also, when we get it up and running, it'll be easier to get ya music out there," Gator said.

"That sounds like a plan. I'll let you know when I can twerk something," C-Lo replied.

Meanwhile, the chicks ease their way up to V.I.P. "Do you have something I can break down this rock with?" Coco asked Tiffany. She had a half of a ball of that good Yayo. You could see the crystal flakes falling off clean through the bag, this was what some called "true fish scale".

"Just use this lighter or your keys. Hurry up before the fellas come up!" Tiffany responded harshly.

16

Coco was her stripper's name, though her real name was Rasheeda, her grandmother named her after her mother died giving birth to her. She had been dancing at Hollywood, the strip club off Columbus Drive, for about six years now, and had a son the same age. And boy was she thicker than all outdoors, short, a little heavy at 190 lbs., but it was in all the right places.

Her baby daddy Dante, aka Fish or Fish Scale, Meatball's brother from Miami, was a known D-boy in Progress Village. He used to treat Coco so bad and never came home at night. In hopes to keep him at home, she started snorting powder with him; it didn't work, he was still in the streets every chance he got. Even though they had been through so much shit, that didn't stop him from being a good father. He was active in his son Lil Divine's life and kept him when Coco had to work.

Nobody around here knew how she got down really, except Tiffany. Mostly because aside from being a big powder head, she was a sight for sore eyes with her short thick legs and long brunette hair that dropped down her back. She was a beautiful redbone with a face like Jada Pinkett-Smith and a bomb body resembling Pinky the Porn Star.

Many niggas had aired her out, but she was still the baddest thing in any club she worked in. Man, did she know how to use what her mother gave her.

Juvenile: *"Girl, you look good, won't you back that azz up*

You'se a fine motherfucker, won't you back that azz up

Call me Big Daddy when you back that azz up!!!"

"Let me use ya card!" Coco said to Tiffany as she smashed down and sniffed a bump, ducking down in V.I.P.

Downstairs, the boyz were having a lot of fun on their own, flirting with all the females in the club. It was ladies' night, so there were plenty to choose from on this Friday night. It was only 10 o'clock and shoulder to shoulder already. While the gang talked to some chicks, C-Lo spotted Capone walk in the front door. Who didn't see him; you couldn't miss him with his multicolored Coogi fit on. C-Lo told his boyz he'd be back.

When he walked over to greet him, he saw Phats with his road dawg Shawn Wilcox, standing on the other side of the open wall, where two fine naked females were in a cage dancing.

Everybody knew Shawn by Dang, short for Danger. He was mischievous, and what you would say, deranged with no remorse. No matter what you decided to call him, something was seriously wrong with the man. He robbed motherfuckers for sport. Nobody knew he had gone to prison for a 30-month bid. He hadn't been back not even a full year and was already on his stick 'em up kid shit. He's the type you must watch; he was grimy and had no fear.

C-Lo had left his Glock in his car. If anything was to kick-off, though, it'd be 15 or 20 niggas on his head, if not more. Still, C-Lo knew he had slipped up. He'd usually just pay the bouncer at every club he went into to hold his toolie. So, imagine, everybody and their mama could be in there strapped if they had the means to grease some hands. Money always talks and bullshit walks.

He proceeded to walk towards Capone as he yelled for him. He never really dealt with him, only through Bam. Capone had been getting so much of his work, they seemed closer than they really were.

"Pone!" C-Lo said.

"What's sup fam! What it be like?" Capone replied.

"You know what it do! Feeling on some booty like R. Kelly, bout to hit V.I.P... Let's get a bottle & rap fool," C-Lo yelled.

"Shh! It's on you?" Capone asked.

C-Lo frowned up his eyebrows, "Man, what you drinking on?"

"That's what I'm talking 'bout! Armadale! Only bring a nigga mo'!"

"Keep it in our reach, daddy!"

They headed up to V.I.P., coping two bottles. When they got there, everybody was already there. Jit-Redd, Rex, Dump, Chief, Cancer, a few others, and the ladies were off in the corner. Coco was getting a lap dance on the red leather sofa by some thick redbone stripper chick, which made C-Lo and Capone's eyes buck, then bust out in laughter.

"So, what's on ya mind with what you was talking about earlier?" Capone asked.

"Look, ya hear me. I got a connect where I can get them thangs at almost twelve to fifteen a block, depends on how many I get. Getting it cheap like that, we can lock down the whole city together," C-Lo answered.

"Man, Lo, with that kind of price and my clientele, it's crazy not to do nothing but get that paper! Shh, I'm with it, but how is this supposed to work?" Capone asked.

"I got two cooks, and it's that true come back so..."

"It ain't that damn good!" Capone cut him off.

"Pone, it's the same coke you been getting from Bam-Bam, that straight pink shish kebab! The streets saying it's the best shit out there right now. My dawg's dad said it's the best he'd tasted in ten years!"

"Shh, I told you what I think. I'm getting mine for double that. So how do you want to do this thang?" Capone replied.

"Look, I'll go get it. He only wants to deal with me. You said you got the clientele, so you just get it from me for the cheap like, and it's so pure you can step on it twice or triple it if you want to! This shit like blue magic nigga!" C-Lo said candidly.

After they worked out some prices, it was official! C-Lo now had him on his team and on top of that, was opening the new traps, sky's the limit! He was only waiting on Santana's call to give the go-ahead on the new operation in their huge apartments. Still, he didn't need any other supplier, or anyone else for that matter, on his team.

He dwelled on what Cancer said earlier but felt like fuck giving up the game because the game had just started.

50 Cent: *"Get Rich, or die trying!"*

While they were holding their meeting, Chief turned towards Cancer as they connected eyes and yelled, "That's our song!" in unison. The club was playing one of their songs from their demo. The sound quality was top notch; it sounded good. They both looked over at C-Lo; he nudged his head with a big Kool-Aid smile as the hook took off.

{Ladies put ya hands on ya knees, bounce that ass and earn dis cheese\ So girl-, shake shake shake and stop- Ma, ma, ma move then drop---, Put ya back into it baby then bring it to the top.}

The hook Cancer had written and put down was just right. Funny thing though, the star on the song wasn't Cancer or C-Lo, but Chief.

{On a late Friday night, these chicks looking thick and right\ Freaks dis dick rock hard, ready to fuck\ Women getting butt-naked, and they bound to twerk, after the show shaking dat azz it's like a thick pillow\ Shh-, boy you know Chief had to follow...}

It was a jam; everyone was super live. (Verse picks up:)

{In the back of the club, she getting love, while BeastMode Rippin da club\ In the club 112 ta the Full Moon Saloon, even suckin it in da afternoon\ So when we get the club crunk, shake rattle and roll--, You in da back with Chief Smokin big blunts of dro- with a bottle in my hand, stand straight-up touch ya toes...} hook starts while he killed his last line. {Then shake like on Earthquake."}

Out of all the bigger names in the building, it was like all eyes were on them based on the way they were performing in VIP! Everybody was having fun. Well, almost everybody. You couldn't see him, but Phats was off in a dark corner with Dang and two females mean mugging. BeastMode was Phats' Label, and Chief talked about the shows and the after-parties when they were together before their falling out. You would think he'd be happy calling or advising, more likely BeastMode Records; guess not, because if looks could kill, C-Lo would have been dead. Phats had a trick for the so-called Boss and his young BMClique...

Chapter 4

"THE WARNING!"

I pulled up at my old apartment I was trapping in. As I got out of my car and wound up towards my apartment, I heard somebody talking about me! It's somebody I knew! Then I heard my boy yell, "C-Lo, watch ya back, that car been parked over there for a long time!"

I head up the stairs to my apartment. As I turned the key to unlock the door, I began to turn the knob. But before I opened it, I looked back at the guy; when I did, I caught him pulling out a gun, only a few steps before reaching the top where I was.

The gunman doesn't hesitate, not giving me one second, he starts to unload on me brutally. I collapsed as the bullets hit me. Two in my left leg, the other in my upper left shoulder. I staggered across the threshold of the doorway bleeding, to death. Then after I fell, the gunman came and stood directly over me. As he yelled something, pointing his gun smack in my face, he began to fire...

"Baby! Baby!" Tiffany screamed at C-Lo.

The gunman pulled the trigger hitting him two more times as he rolled on his right side, facing her, yelling, "Don't shoot! Please! Don't shoot me No more!"

"Baby! Baby! C-Lo! Wake up, baby! Wake up, what you dreaming about?"

He sat up quickly, analyzing where he was, fresh out his dream in a heavy cold sweat.

"You okay, baby?"

"It was so real, babe!" he replied.

"It was only a dream, baby!"

"I know, but it didn't feel like it, it was so real! Remember when I stayed in Pebble-Wood on 52nd & Fowler?"

"Yea!"

"It was somebody I knew. They told me about some car that I think had followed me to the apartments, then had ducked off in the parking lot."

"Okay," she said, nodding for him to keep going.

"Listen! I headed to the front door, and after I put the key in, some dude that had followed me up the stairs shot me! I can't pinpoint who it was, but when I got hit, I felt every bullet burn through my flesh!"

C-Lo examined the air blankly, rubbing on his side and the over his head, and his brain stopped for a moment, "It's somebody I know!"

"It was only a dream, baby. Want to talk about it?"

"Naw, I got to get up anyway," he said as he yawned and stretched for the ceiling. "I got to get up. It's gone be a long day.

**

A week had gone by; it was Friday again. C-Lo's vacation was over, he had got that call from his connect, so it was time to get that work. As he sat on the end of his bed, he reached for his half of blunt and fired it up, thinking while his mentor's song silently played in his head.

2-pac "I see death around the corner. Gotta stay high. Will I survive in the city where the skinny nigga's die! If they bury me, bury me as a "G" Nigga!!!"

He got ready while Tiffany sprung downstairs and cooked them breakfast. As he showered, his iPhone rang. C-Lo jumped out to catch it; before the lyrics from Floetry's *"Say Yes"* went off, he double-checked but already knew it was his sister Angel. "Sis!" he recited under his breath after seeing the missed call notification. He jumped back in the shower and finished up.

After he got out, Tiffany didn't give him a chance to get dressed fully before calling him to come down.

"Baby, you ready to eat?"

"Yea! I'll be down in a minute!"

He quickly brushes his teeth then dial's his sister, Angel. Angel is seven years older than C-Lo, with a hood-ass teenager named Jasmine, but most called her lady, short for Ladyhood. His sister favored him tremendously. They had different dads but could go for twins, just like their mom dukes.

A sexy caramel little thing she was, but a tower at 6'3 feet tall. She was slim built, long lanky petite legs with a globe-shaped jello butt, tiny 26" waist, and short curly hair that would be any color on any given day.

An athletic sister and one hell of an athlete like her two brothers. She played basketball at Chamberlain High School and through her college ball years at the University of South Florida. She was captain of her team and led them in points and rebounds.

The scouts were looking for her to be drafted first or second to Candice Parker until she hurt her left knee in a championship title game from a bad fall her junior year in college. It was a disappointment she didn't make it to the WNBA. She was that talented.

She now works for the City of Tampa's Water Department but lives in Haines City out in Polk County, Florida, in a $250,000 two-bedroom house. She has a 7-series Benz, a brand-new Lexus, and a big girl pink and scarlet "06" Tahoe truck sitting kind of high outside.

The chick had her priorities together and didn't need to ask her older brother C-Lo for nothing. One thing she didn't do was let her family know much about her personal relationships.

She never mentioned her male friends, which she didn't have many of anyway. So, most of her relatives and friends thought she was a lesbian.

"Hey, big bruh?"

"Hey, sis! I saw you called me, but I was in the shower getting ready to leave. What's really good, doe?"

"Getting ready myself. You still driving that Waste Management truck?"

"Yea. Well, kinda part-time."

"That's good. I didn't want anything. I was just chilling. I did have to go get Mama from work this morning. Her car didn't want to start. Besides that, I was just thinking about you."

"She aight?"

"Oh, yea, you aight? You sound kinda down, Mann!" Mann was his nickname his family had been calling him since he was 3 years old.

"I'm fine. I just had one of my bad dreams," C-Lo replied.

"You still having that one dream where you fell in a deep black hole and never got out?" She laughs.

"It's just not a deep hole, it's a deep mass grave...cause I couldn't get out, like that's where I die at...and no. It was a different one. What's the 4-1-1 on Mama's whip?"

"Oh, I'm taking it to the shop to get it fix this afternoon, again. So, how's that good for nothin' chick of yours?" she asks.

"Come on, Angelina. I never understood why you don't like her!"

Just as he finished his sentence, Tiffany walked in with a crazy look on her face. "You coming down to eat or what? Your food getting cold!" she said in a nasty attitude.

"Yea! Here I come babe!" As she walks out the door, Angel begins talking again.

"Angelina! So, what you call ya-self mad na? You never call me by my real name!"

"I'm not mad, but..."

"You should be, cause she don't do a damn thang for you. All she does is sit on her plump azz and spend up ya money on her nails and her hair! Have she found another job yet?"

"Come on, Sis! Look how you acting! You can't do that; that's not fair."

"What you mean not fair! She don't help you, and I know it!"

"That right there shows you what you know, and if I'm happy, why you can't be happy for me?"

"Yea! Okay! You know I love you, but I don't have to deal with her!"

"Okay, you think! I hope she's gone be ya sister-n-law soon!"

"Whatever negro!" Angel says. He laughs. "Not my sister-in-law!"

C-Lo laughed again, "You better get used to it but look, ya hear me?"

"Yea!"

"Let me finish eating and getting ready, so I can leave. I'll hit you and call Mama later, K?"

"Okay, Man! Love You!"

"Love you too, Sis..."

C-Lo filed downstairs to eat. Tiffany was at the kitchen table, sitting there staring at both plates on the table. She looks up at him for a split second with that look you have before you go shoot up a bank or your old job where you just got fired from, like a mad man.

"What you want to drink?" she asked in a rough tone.

"OJ," CJ replied.

She went to retrieve the jug to pour two glasses of Orange Juice for them to drink while asking, "Who was that blowing ya phone up?"

C-Lo replied, "My sister. Mama's car stopped again. She was calling to tell me and to see how we were doing."

"We!" she said sarcastically, rolling her eyes as she picked up her fork to poke at her cold eggs. He didn't know if she'd overheard him on the phone or not, but that was the last thing he needed to be worried about at the time. He had bigger fish to fry today.

It was cold silence while they ate. C-Lo jumped back and forth. He finished scraping his plate, then kissed her, "I love you."

"I love you too, baby, but we need to have a talk."

"Talk! Bout what?" C-Lo asked.

"It can wait. Just be careful out there, baby."

With that said, he grabbed his bag & his Glock seventeen before storming out the door. He jumped in his apple red Benz and called his man Sam-Bam as he pulled off.

"Hello?"

"Sammy boy!"

"What's Poppin Lo?"

"Paper Chasing! Bout to B-line down to Channel-side blood, to handle that buzz with Momondo. I also got to go holla at Meatball and them boyz about them apartments we trying to put on lock."

"Damn all that, ha?"

"Yea, and a few more stops before I even go down bottom to have lunch.

"You got enough time to swing through to get that?" Sam said.

"Naw! That will be doubling back, but I'll come through so we can talk bout that and tell you what's up with that other stuff when I get back from doing that."

28

"Bet that up, Blood, do that!"

"Superb then, fool!" Bam said.

"Superb B!"

Bam hung up the phone in a hurry to make another call to his side chick. When she picked up, she went off. "Why in the hell are you calling me and while I'm at the house too! Is you slow, or just that dumb? C-Lo could have been standing right here next to me! You could have sent me a text or something!" Tiffany said, pissed after seeing the caller ID.

"Calm down, lady. I know he ain't there. He just called me and told me he was on his way to meet somebody down at the bottom and have lunch or some shit! So do you want to go get a bite or go for drinks or something?"

"Damn right!"

"I'll be ready in 30!"

"Okay, meet me at our spot."

TLC: "So I creep! Yeaaa… Just Creepin on down low. Nobody has to know…"

***

"The Cheater"

Tiffany got ready and left. On the way to their spot, she never noticed she was being followed by somebody in a black vehicle.

When they got to the Golden Corral on 56th North Fowler, they parked side by side. They talked briefly and ended up agreeing on not going in for food or drinks, only because they'd started kissing in his car. She started sucking on his bottom lip as their passion entwined. In the middle of doing so, he put his hand between her warm thighs, and that was it.

"Come on, let's go!" she lecherously said, jumping out his and in her car. She followed him to his apartment complex that was right around the corner in Terrace Point. After jumping out of their vehicles, they immediately met up at his front door and picked up where they left off, lip-locking as Bam opened the door.

When they finally got inside, the door hadn't even closed well before they both clawed at each other. Tiffany roughly rubbed her palm across his crotch and started playing with his meat. He was so excited she could feel him bulging through his jeans. He yanked her blouse right over her head with ease. She unfastened his skull belt, unzipped his pants, and whipped out his monster. As his pants plopped to the floor, her eyes got big as a blowfish like she'd seen nothing like it before. He was hung, very comparable to a horse, and it was already hard as could be.

While they kissed, she rubbed and tugged smoothly on his package. She'd rode him briskly and wild while he caressed her ass and squeezed repeatedly. He swiftly unclipped her bra and watched as her perfectly shaped breasts flopped out as two healthy overweight water balloons.

He started sucking and licking on her quarter-size nipples until he saw them point at him. She bent straight down, squatting almost on her knees, and put his enormous juicy rod inside of her mouth.

"Oh-shit, yeah..." He squealed as she maneuvered her warm tongue identical to a snake. Slobbing, slowly licking both sides of his baton while playing with his almonds, simultaneously deep throating his love stick, gobbling his whole thing, making it disappear in her warm bragger. She repeated this again and again, feeling his intensity throbbing in between her moist lips, knowing any moment his eagerness was going to erupt spontaneously with pleasure.

Her twat was wet. She was full of desire from amusing the thought of Bam deep off inside of her. She leaped up, grabbing his hand. "Come on!" she uttered in an attractive voice. They left the foyer and went to the bedroom hand and hand. She knew exactly where it was from being there more than a handful of times. She led him until she fell ass first on the bed. He weltered her legs up in the air and drove headfirst into her po-nanny, hungry as a lesbian. He stroked his dick back and forth as he suctioned her kitty-cat, acting as if it was a sweet piece of candy on the roof of his mouth.

She could tell he was a pro himself the way he gently licked and munched at her clit. She grabbed his long dreads on the side of his head that was wrested up in two hair ties and rolled her head viciously while blinking her eyes as he suctioned her kitty-cat, acting as if it was a sweet piece of candy on the roof of his mouth. He swiftly unclipped her bra and watched as her perfectly shaped breasts flopped out as two healthy overweight water balloons. He started sucking and licking on her quarter-size nipples until he saw them point at him.

"Oh yeah, oh yeah!!" she moaned loudly at the peak of her delight, having an orgasm after he'd slid all his overhung black staff in and out of her pretty pink thang.

She was unbelievably ready for another as he went in and out of her juicy twat. She'd rode him briskly and wild while he caressed her ass and squeezed repeatedly. He was penetrating her with deep thrusts bringing her onto rapture. They continued to fuck for about another 20 to 25 minutes until their bodies reached the point of ecstasy while he was deep inside of her.

Chapter 5

"THE MEETING"

C-Lo made a few stops. First, he met with Rex and Meatball and dropped them four bricks. He was ready to help supply a major apartment complex, but were they? With the type of plan, they had contracted for this trap and the area in general, the BMClique was going to get off enough snow to make the summer look like Christmas.

The BMC Boyz were about to take off. They were packaging up, getting ready to open the door to move the first shipment, and were just waiting for C-Lo's call. After he met up with them, he went and dropped Fish, Coco's baby daddy, some work and picked up some money he'd owed him. He then headed towards downtown.

It was creeping up on 12:30 when he called Santana, his Colombian connect that he called Mexico. Santana picked up, "Que Pasa!"

"Hey, amigo! Como Esta?" C-Lo said.

Santiago laughed, "I'm doing good, my friend!"

"Alright, I should be pulling up in a short minute."

"Okay, my friend, I'll see you when you get by K?"

Minutes later, C-Lo rode past Hooter's on Channel-side and observed him at a table on the outside patio with another Spanish guy having a drink. He turned in, parked, and headed inside. He stopped at the bar, copped him a tall shot glass of Grey Goose, then proceeded to the patio where they were seated.

C-Lo sat down before Santana could finish saying, "Sit-down... What's good, my friend?"

"You! Let's get down to business! Who this?" C-Lo said kind of harsh.

"That's why I like you, my friend. You always about business before pleasure!"

"And!"

"Okay, Buey, let's talk business then. First of all, never talk to me like you fuckin crazy ever again in ya entire life, in less you ready to die!" Santana laughed to himself, only showing half a smile. "Second of all, this is my brother Rico. This is who's supplying you with what you need!"

Rico, Santana's older brother, supplied most of the southeast and the east coast, helping three percent of the cocaine and heroin coming into America. That is with him teaming up with his brother, who floods mainly the northern to the central part of Florida and half of Texas.

C-Lo met Santana two years ago through a Hispanic cat buying gray bricks of that "roin"; he introduced the two. C-Lo had been getting work from him for over a year now.

C-Lo blew a gasket. "So, what, I need a co-signer now?"

"Mild down and shut up sometimes, k, Buey!"

C-Lo felt Santana was getting besides himself since his brother was present, but that was the last straw. He pulls out his Glock seventeen and put in on the table. C-Lo cocked back the hammer, leaving it flat on the table. "Yeah, whatever, man! Na, you talking reckless! I know that, and you damn sho' know that!" C-Lo stared off with a murderous look in his eyes, "You not the only one that drops bodies Nig, really tho! Let's get this straight, na!"

Rico takes a quick look at the two tables next to them. Seated are two broad chests Puerto Ricans with guns pointed at C-Lo hidden underneath their tables.

"This is not why we came here! Are we good, Buey?" Santana asked.

"Listen here! Ya hear me! This how I eat! This how I live, that Scarface shit don't scare me!" They looked at each other.

"We don't do business like this! It's supposed to be me and you! What if I would have shown up with somebody you didn't know?"

Santana spoke with calmness. "I get that point dearly! Don't worry about that! Just hear him out."

"I'm good like my money. So, what you got to say?" C-Lo responded, putting his pistol back in his waistline.

"Okay, C-Lo, I would have probably done the same thing if I was in your shoes, that's all understandable. But understand, I had to come so you meet me and hear me out," Rico said.

"I hear ya!"

"I can't front you fifty keys."

"What! I knew it was gonna be some shit in da game! You had me come all the way down here fa this!"

35

"Slow down, Lo! Let him finish!" Santana half snapped.

Rico continued, "Only way I can front you fifty is if you fifty!"

"How much?" C-Lo quickly responded interestedly.

"Twelve apiece. After you finish paying us what you owe, you can get them for the ten-five." "Ten-five?"

"Yea, ten thousand five hundred!"

C-Lo paused and did the quick math in his head. It was along short silence while he played with $600,000...

Santana broke everybody's meditation. "If that's too steep for you, we can always do twenty-five front twenty-five at twenty..."

"Naw! I can handle the fifty! So, when will they be ready?"

"Now, meet us at our club in Ybor City called Empire on 7th at 8pm."

"I know where it's at!"

"Well, don't be late then! Call us when you get there. I'll have someone show you when you arrive. Come by yourself and please don't try no Billy-the-kid stunts, or I will kill you, ya wife, and everybody you fuckin care about! Especially if you ever pull a pistol on me again! I really hope you understand this...do right by us, and we will take care of you and ya whole family."

"Yea, okay! Like I told you," Santana looked into C-Lo's eyes all cherished, and after a pause, C-Lo finished his sentence, "I don't even like Billy-Da-Kid! I gotcha, Amigo!"

It was fifteen minutes till one when C-Lo jumped in his whip. He relaxed his head on the headrest, reflecting on what just happened. He opened his eyes, put his Glock in between the seat, fired up half a blunt, and smirked as he popped in his Jeezy cd.

"Snowman nigga, just remember the name..." He turned the key and bobbed his head, listening. *"Check ya watch nigga, it's my time!!!"* He slightly became amused pulling off because now he was the snowman, and he was about to make it snow. C-Lo went and picked up all the money he had stashed at Raven's house before heading home. but forgot he had to stop at Bam's house.

Chapter 6

"THE YEGG"

Back at Bam's place, he and Tiffany were lying in bed, wet from sweaty sex. They both panted so loud, sounding exhausted from a long run. After catching their breath, Tiffany rolled over and glanced at her phone. "Holy shit! I didn't know it was this late! I gotta go!" She quickly jumped up, rushed into the bathroom and hopped in to take a quick shower. When she finished getting ready, she kissed Bam on his forehead as they said their goodbyes, and she rushed out the door.

Seconds later, Bam got out of his waterbed and stumbled directly into the master bathroom, nude with a smile from ear to ear, because he had been knocking his best friend C-Lo's back out fiancé' for over 6 months right under his nose. While he was taking a piss, he heard his front door close.

"Ha, ha, ha… you back for round two already?" He chuckled out with an even more lop-sided grin. He just knew Tiffany had to forget something. He just knew it. Who else it could have been when he didn't hear a response, he rinsed his hands off, then exited the bathroom? As he did, his phone rang.

"It's Boss-hog! Who the Boss Nigga! Who the motherfuckin Boss! Who the...?" It was C-Lo, he knew from the ringtone.

"You know C-Lo should be heading this way in... Aye! Oh-shit." Bam had run smack into a tall, masked man, with shiny steel pointed directly at him, blocking his sight.

"Motherfucker, you got ya hands up like you ready to play stupid nigga! Where it's at?" the masked man asked.

"How the fuck you get in here? She let you in?" Bam asked dramatically.

The yegg instantly shot Bam in his ventral, causing blood to gush from his belly, collapsing him to his knees. "Oh, Lord!"

"Yea, that's what they call him! So, saying that I'm kind of in a rush, let me ask the questions in this bitch...and I'm only gone ask you one mo' time, or the lord you just met will be the one getting you to cooperate! Where it's at?"

Bam laid on the floor winded and in pain. "In the safe, everything is in the safe," he said slowly and painfully.

"Where's the safe at, dumbass?"

"In the closet! Fuck!!! In the back of the closet!" Bam sobbed, clutching his stomach.

" Now that's mo' like it! Well, nigga, what you waiting on, a fuckin invitation! Get dere! Oh yea! I ain't with all that funny shit either. I swear, try some heroic shit you want to mane, and you won't see New Year's cause I'm gonna cancel ya Christmas!"

The robber followed Bam to the closet and opened the medium-sized box safe that was cheap, unhidden and unlocked. When the yegg opened it, he found nearly 80 something stacks and four bricks of pure cocaine. "Tighten down nigga! Throw all them goodies in the bag!" Bam had no choice and did what was told of him, hearing his cellular ring again.

"It's Bosshog! What the Boss nigga! Who the motherfuckin Boss! Who the Boss nigga!!!"

He filled and dragged the bag out of the closet while he continued to clutch his stomach. The gunman had his lord draped with a silencer pointing it at him the whole time. Out of nowhere, the yegg removed his mask.

Bam whispered, "Danger."

"Yea Fuck-boy, you can thank C-Lo for the baptism!" He said right before he pulled the trigger to his lord uncontrollably, you might know Smith and Wesson. He put two bullets in the head, a third lonely one went through his neck, spattering blood all over the carpet and across the bed. He laughed at how every time the virtual power of his lord made niggas get down or act right and lay down.

If you didn't catch it, it was Phats' right-hand man Dang. He had been paid to eliminate C-Lo. Tiffany was followed from her house, expecting she would lead Dang to C-Lo. Dang was wrong, but it still worked out for him. He found it amusing that he had lucked up on an even greater target and loss to C-Lo, his #1-Man. The day started out to be wonderful, at least for Dang.

***

The Finding

Shortly after C-Lo came from Raven's place, it was one o'clock on the dot. As he rode up 22nd, he called Bam. The phone just rang, but minutes later, he tapped his Bluetooth to try again, sitting at the light on 22nd and Hillsborough Ave with no luck. So, he called Capone.

"Hello?"

"What dey do?"

"That's what I was about to ask you! You ready for me?" C-Lo asked.

"Most def, it just went down. Let's meet at ten, so we can finish talkin' business." "Aight! Whereat? On 40th, at the bar."

"The Apollo?" Capone questioned.

"Yea, that way, we can have a drink first."

"Aight then, Bet that up. Hit me later."

"Aight... A Pone!"

"What's up?"

"You talked to Bam Bam?"C-Lo asked.

"Naw, not since what, Saturday."

"Damn, six days ago!" he repeated to himself and then said, "Superb Fool!"

"Superb!" Capone said and hung up.

C-Lo hung up and tried Bam again. After yet another tries with no luck, he decided to stop by his place anyway since he was already coming up 56th street on his way home. First, he calls Tiffany right before pulling into Bam's apartments, just missing a black car turning out his apartments wildly.

"Hey, baby."

"Hey babe...Damn!" He screamed at the car that almost collided with him.

"What's wrong, baby?"

"This ugly green car almost hit me! It's nothin', I'm good. I'm on my way home. Want me to stop anywhere before I get there?"

"Naw baby! I'm not home anyways. I'm with Coco getting my nails and hair did." But really, at that time, she'd just pulled up at the salon all by herself from just leaving Bam's place minutes before.

"I should be done in a few hours, but if you need me, I'm up on 50th and Busch at the shop. You straight though, baby?"

"Yea, I just wanted to let you know everything went superb, and I love the shit out cha," C-Lo said, parking next to Bam's car in front of his apartment.

"Awe, I love you too, Pookie!"

He laughed. "Hahaha! You crazy girl. Call me when you on ya way."

She laughed too, "Hahaha, okay."

As C-Lo walked in the direction of Bam's door, he knew he was home because his candy-painted vermillion reddish orange "eighty-eight" Regal was parked in his parking spot. When he gets to the door, he sees it is opened. He writhed left and right, then looked back at the door. His face had a concrete sign of confusion written all over it. He made sure his Glock seventeen was off the safety as he gradually pushed open the door more and entered.

"Bam-Bam!" C-Lo whooped, stepping only one foot across the threshold. "Bam-Bam!" He extended his gun, stepping fully into the apartment, which was clean like his man always kept it. It wasn't anything out of place as far as he could tell, but he caught a funny whiff floating in the air. *"Sex!"* No, it was something else, and something felt wrong, making him think of his dream from that morning.

He quickly threaded through the foyer and into the small living room, passing Tupac, Lil Wayne, and Scarface pictures. "Bam-Bam!" There was no answer and still no sign of a break-in or any indication of the trouble that was about to strike him.

When he toured the hallway, he'd been alerted by a lamp that laid on the bedroom floor as he adventured on, his heart stopped. "Bam, Bam...No Bam!" C-Lo yelled frantically, finding his best friend's naked body in a fresh pool of blood. He bent over and took his pulse. As he did, his head plunged over stiffly.

He was still warm, shockingly, with his brains exiting multiple sides of his head. He could taste the corpse. Everything had taken place in the bedroom, a terrible mess similar to the mad max in Top Shottas. It was much worse than anything he'd ever seen or imagined.

"Got damn! Look at all this blood everywhere," he said out loud to himself before he quickly snapped his neck to look over his shoulder. He heard something. "Oh shit, the police! No, the killer still here!" he thought. He jumped up in a panic and checked the first bedroom, then the second bedroom with his gun cocked, drawn, and ready without a soul to be found.

He knew Bam always held his dope and stuff inside a mini-safe inside his closet. So, he rushed to check it...only to find it wide open and empty. No work, no money, no nothing! He stopped to calculate the situation but couldn't from being traumatized.

"Bam's dead. I can't believe this shit! I can't just leave him here naked, soaking in his own blood like this." He fought to keep his cool but couldn't help continuously freaking out. His best friend had been robbed, killed, and left for the vultures; two shots to the head, close-in, execution-style.

"I can't call the police," He sighed heavily. The police might be on their way anyways if they didn't use a silencer or if someone had seen me coming here with my pistol out. A half a second passed, then he took another deep breath. "Fuck it!" He picked up the house phone with the corner of his shirt and called 911.

The operator picked up, "911, what's your emergency?"

"I just found my friend shot! I think he's dead!"

"Stay calm, sir!"

The lady asked him the address and a series of questions. When she asked him his name, he hung up in her face and began to run out, when out of his peripheral vision next to the phone, he sees a diamond ring.

The gold ring that caught his eye looked familiar. He froze up as he held it, knowing he knew where it was from. He started having crazy thoughts but couldn't dwell on them because he could hear sirens coming from a distance. He cuffed the ring, dropped it in his pocket, and shot out.

Chapter 7

"REMINISCENT"

While driving up Fowler Ave, minutes away from his house, C-Lo stops at a red light, pulls out the ring, and glances at it. He flipped it and looked inside. After a swift examination, he sees the inscription that reads: "Luv TT" engraved inside it.

"What the fuck!" It's the ring he personally had made for Tiffany and gave it to her on one of their anniversaries. TT is her initials. C-Lo sunk into a trance and started to reminisce.

***

Tony Toni Tone: "Do you know what today is? It's our Anniversary!"

It was C-Lo and Tiffany's 2nd Anniversary. They'd gone to Orlando, Florida, for a week of fun in the sun. They didn't have as much money at the time, but enough to put a smile on her face. He rented a villa on International Drive in a suburban residence. They dressed up and went to Disney World, Magic Kingdom, Sea World, Universal Studios, and some NBA stores with old-school collectible items. There he had pictures taken of him and put on the covers of magazines. One cover was of ESPN; it read: "Charles, #1 Draft pick of the year!" One of the

Slam magazines read, "Rookie of the Year, Charles!" Both were excellent headlines with him holding a basketball with a #1 Chicago Bulls jersey on.

They talked about his dreams while there and had the time of their lives. in a suburban residence. One thing she got for C-Lo was an all-diamond C-shaped key chain; you could see it from a distance. It shined so bright in the light it sparkled; they even got matching fits to attend the Epcot Center and dined at some of the lavish 5-star restaurants in the city: breakfast in bed, all you can eat buffets and all kinds of things. They also took pictures non-stop all day long. It was a time to remember. He couldn't forget how great of a time they had.

C-Lo had a ring specially made for Tiffany by Tiffany and Co. Their last night in Orlando was one to remember. He had grapes and all various types of sliced and diced fruits, with a neat, unique shaped bottle of Stolichnaya Elite, the finest Russian Vodka. He had wrapped it all in a unique ice bucket with a red ribbon around it and a big red bow.

The night was planned out wonderfully, but he had to find some way to get her out of the room so he could finish staging a romantic scene. He came up with an idea. He pretended like he had a migraine from hell, so she took a trip to Walgreens to get him some headache medication.

While she was gone, that gave him enough time to lace a hot bubble bath with red rose petals leading from the front door to the bedroom and to the tub. After he scattered more rose petals all over the bed and inside the tub, he rolled a blunt and waited.

That night was special, the whole entire trip, for that matter. It turned out to be something extraordinary. Everything was perfect for when she came back. As soon as she turned the corner and walked back in, she was shocked out of this world and completely caught off guard. He got on one knee in the middle of the rose petals and asked for her hand in marriage. That's when he had gifted her the specialized 2 karat diamond ring.

He had some baby-making CDs made up; slow jams entertained them the whole night. He had planned to get her pregnant that night; it would've made the night and trip even more special. As they slid in the oversize granite-like black marble Jacuzzi, Jodeci's *Feenin* was playing. They smoked a blunt while playing with the bubbles, talking, and laughing. Once they started kissing and incorporating the fruit, the foreplay began.

They were arousing each other to the highest point of pleasure, and that carried straight into the bedroom. C-Lo massaged her down, starting with the back of her lower neck, working her slowly from head to toe. He pulled a can of whipped cream right out of the dorm refrigerator next to the side of the bed. He tried to lick it off of every inch of her body. When he got to her navel, he stopped then continued slowly towards her pussycat until her legs quivered uncontrollably.

He took a cherry off some cream that sat on her stomach, bit it, and used it to seduce her clitoris. She moaned wildly for him to stop, and when he didn't, she exploded into body-twitching orgasms.

R Kelly: *"Come over here and let me take off your clothes/ Cause things I want to do to you nobody has to know!"*

Just hearing her wail made his dick hard. In the few years they had been together at the time, never once had they tried the sex position sixty-nine. They didn't even know how they fell

47

into it. He slipped his fingers in and out her dripping wet good stuff while he softly tickled her clit with his crafty tongue. She soaked up his overgrown shaft, slowly licking up one side then the next by suctioning, cupping down the other. It seemed to be even more like a popsicle than a lollipop adventure with her sparkling lips on it. Tiffany had everything saturated from her dripping pussy to her masterful head job. C-Lo never had seen the tricks she had mastered on him. She continued to slob and rub her tongue back and forth across the tip of his erection.

She always did this move when she was about to climax where she'd shake her legs all the way down to her ankles and wiggle her toes, trying to push him off. Then admittedly pushed his head down, running away from him eating her kitty cat. C-Lo wasn't playing fair himself. Tonight, he wasn't backing away until she was about to bust a mess. He wanted her to ooze all over his dick, not knowing it was half too late.

As he caressed her love box with both his tongue and his fingertips, he felt her G-Spot tighten up on top of him. He wasn't allowing her to get up or push away just yet.

"Oh-Lord! Yes!" she screamed. A few moments later, letting him know she was on the verge of climax. He quickly slid from underneath her without her budging, reached her back from behind, then swiftly thrust his wet dick inside her doggie-style. She clawed at the sheets while taking every inch of what he was giving her. As soon as he plowed off inside of her, she squealed like a virgin and oozed all over his swollen shaft as planned. He grasped her booty cheeks and continued to mound her like an animal in several positions.

"Uh oh, you a beast! Don't stop! Oh yes! Please don't stop!" She was about to repeat another orgasm minutes apart. "I'm about to cum! Don't stop! She was so loud that the neighbors had to know. Both of them had buckets of sweat everywhere before he hymned and climaxed inside of her, as she exploded into body-twitching orgasms.

C-Lo's mind went haywire. "Why the fuck was her engagement ring at Sam-Bam's place?" he wondered. "Damn, did she set him up? Was she just fucking with him? Or was it both?"

Chapter 8

"CONFRONT?"

C-Lo can't seem to get the thought of Tiffany betraying him out of his head; his mind is stuck, moving in circles. Wondering why and how the hell Bam got knocked off and what Tiffany had to do with it? that part was making him looney trying to figure out he had a brain fart. "Coco! What did she know?" he thought to himself.

They had been friends way before Tiffany had even thought about coming to Tampa. It was never a sexual thing between them by far. He had never seen her that way. She was very sexy but not his type. Mostly because she was wide open. I'll say it, a whore! Plain and simple. She was a busy body and had been with too many men, and most of them he knew.

He picked up his iPhone and scrolled down his contacts. He went through the phone contacts and thought about her ringtone: 2-Pac's: *Wonder Why They Call You Bitch*. He called her, since she was supposedly with Tiffany, so she says.

"Hey, big bruh! What's going on, baby boy?" Coco said with excitement, answering her big pretty glistening phone on the first ring. C-Lo responded, "Nothin'! Have you seen Tiff?"

"No, not since the club last weekend. I talked to her yesterday, though."

"Why, what's wrong?"

C-Lo replied, "I need to tell you something but didn't want her next to you and me just calling you out of the blue like something going on between me and you. I don't have time for the bullshit. That's the last thing a brother needs right now."

"I feel ya. What's on your mind, big bruh?" Coco asked.

C-Lo closed his eyes and paused.

"What's wrong, baby boy?" she asked.

He almost shed a tear, "Bam-Bam is dead, as in gone...not breathing. I stopped by his house before I went home and found him. I called the police and everything, but I got ghost before they got there."

She paused, not believing what she was hearing. "WHAT HAPPENED?"

C-Lo answered, "I don't know, baby girl, but he'd been shot, and blood was all over the place. It was gross, Coco. I've never seen anything like it in my life."

"Woow! Oh my God! Woow! Tiff knows?" Coco screamed.

C-Lo answered, "No, that's why I was calling you. She didn't pick up her phone."

"She told me she had to get her hair done. She might be at the shop already," she said.

"I think so too. I'm about to hit her again. I just figured she was with you," C-Lo replied.

"Naw, I told her I wasn't going Wednesday. No, I meant yesterday. You okay though?"

"Besides finding my best friend dead with his brains bled out, literally, I'm Gucci!" he answered sarcastically.

"I'm just saying, I know you," she said curiously.

"Yea, I know... me too. But I don't know who, why or what happened, but believe when I do find out..." C-Lo said almost going into a daydream.

"When you do find out, don't do nothing idiotic big bruh!" Coco yelled.

"I'm a big boy. I'm gonna be good, good, trust! I'm about to call my girl. Sister don't tell her I hit cha. Like I said, I don't want her tripping. I don't know how she's going to act. You know how women can get. I want to be the first to tell her." C-Lo said.

"Okay, baby boy, I gotcha. Call me later and for God's sake, stay out of trouble!" "Alright, sis."

They both simultaneously hung up. C-Lo blew his top, becoming angry that Tiffany had lied and wasn't with Coco like she said she was. He knocked over a picture of him and her sitting next to their bed as it broke onto the floor. "Why? WHY? Why you LIED to me about something so little for?" he said, zigzagging as he paced the floor, burning a hole in the carpet, becoming angrier and even more suspicious. He'd contemplated what he would do about that worthless slut for lying to him and sleeping with not just any nigga, but his so-called best friend.

He gathered up enough nerve to call and confront her. Tiffany picked up her Galaxy Note, almost damaging her wet nails about to get under the hairdryer, getting her other hand-painted. "Hey baby," she expressed genuinely after stopping Plies' ringtone: *"Asked her what da problem...she said you fuckin awesome!..."*

Looking down at her hand, she noticed that one of her rings was missing as her nails were getting done.

"Don't hey baby me, bitch! So how long you been fuckin Bam, hoe?" is what C-Lo wanted to say, but instead desperately wanted to see her reaction when he told her Bam was dead. "Hey Bae, I just got home a minute ago. You know how long you and Coco gonna be before y'all finish up?" he asked.

"I'll be finished in an hour. They already finished our nails and feet and working on our hair now. Why? What's wrong, baby? You sound down. You still thinking about your dream from this morning?" Tiffany asked.

That had escaped his mind. His dream was probably a red stop sign. A vision from God, a warning that Bam was about to get popped. It kind of felt like Deja Vu when she said that. C-Lo replied, "I found Bam today at his apartment." She got nervous about waiting on what he was referring to, knowing she'd not too long ago left Bam.

"What you mean?" she replied.

"What you mean what I mean, I found him dead," C-Lo answered.

"WHAT! Why you gotta be fucking playing like that all the time, Charles!" Tiffany responded frantically.

He couldn't pinpoint if she was trying to sound misleading or not but he could tell immediately that she couldn't believe him.

She knew something. He didn't trust her, or anyone else for that matter, anymore.

"Right after I called you, I was at his place and found him in a giant pool full of blood by his bedside DEAD!!!" C-Lo yelled.

She became nerveless and got all shaky like she hoped he was lying. "I just left there twenty minutes ago," Tiffany thought to herself. "You have got to be kidding me! What the police say?" she asked.

"I called them when I found him, but I hit it," C-Lo responded.

From that statement, she knew right then he wasn't bullshitting. "I'll be home in a second," she uttered hastily. She hung up, not waiting on his reply. She went straight into a panic state. "I can't believe this shit. Whoever it was probably waited on me to leave. That means the killer knows who I am, and I was having sex with him. Were they hiding in his place the whole time? Oh, my lord, my DNA gone pop-up everywhere! Did someone see me leave his place? If C-Lo just left there around the time he called me, did he see me? Or just missed me? Better yet, the killer."

All kinds of scenarios went through her head while she drove to the house, pulling out her hair. "Where in the hell is my ring!" She didn't even remember she left her ring on Bam's nightstand next to his bed; she was terrified and in shock. She was stuck, but she knew C-Lo wasn't that kind of man...but he was.

He got the impression from their fast connection that she really didn't have anything to do with the homeboy's death, but that could only mean she was just screwing him. Yeah, just screwing him! He tried to think just because he found the ring over

54

there, it didn't mean she was either. Which he knew was a bunch of shit but gave her a slight benefit of the doubt.

His mind jumped, puzzling, and coming to a sudden halt. "What if the police find my fingerprints or my DNA all over Bam's place? Shit, what if they find hers?" He collapsed in his chair as he tracked out his thoughts and rolled a fat blunt to calm his nerves.

Later after getting his mind right, he called many BM and liquor, his brother, Cancer, and Capone. Capone intended to find out who killed his roe-dog and was anticipating hog-tying and addressing anybody he had simple arguments with. Everyone was mainly shocked at the news. Bam didn't have any enemies. C-Lo's mind couldn't help but wander off thinking how on a serious note if he would've caught him and Tiffany having sex, he would have killed them both right where he found them.

Thirty minutes had gone by before Tiffany got to the house. She went straight upstairs to their master bedroom, where he was taking a hot bath, smoking on another blunt, and drinking on a fifth of a Crown Royal straight out of the bottle, getting wasted. She entered through their beautifully decorated green and black bedroom and into their equally beautiful bathroom, attempting to hug and kiss him. He sat all the way up in the specially made green marble tub breaking his neck to see if her ring was on her hand or not. He wanted to think differently about the situation but already knew the truth.

He watched her kneel, throw together her half-ass did hair, and noticed two rings on her right hand, but none on the other. She was missing her engagement ring, of course, because he had found it. He dodged her hug and kiss, looking away. His mind was unstoppable from wanting to hurt her so bad. He tried to block out the evil thoughts that strolled across his brainwaves. In between being half-drunk already and having bricks of cocaine in the house, he played it smooth, plus knowing that he'd beat her shitless, she might call the police on him.

"I just need to be by myself right now so I can clear my head." He lightly pushed her away. No matter the situation, she still loved him and wanted to comfort him when needed. She saw the half-empty bottles and figured he'd instead embraced it than her. So, she decided to leave him welling on his solitude.

The truth was, he wasn't sure he'd ever trust her again; speaking another word about love right now would be absurd.

***

"Sex on Point"

A little while later, Cancer, Chief, and 5P came through. When they got there, C-Lo was straight booked and had cracked a fifth of Crown. All of them sat in the studio talking about what happened to Bam, coming up with different possible scenarios.

Cancer had an instrumental playing the entire time; he'd been working on it for over a week now. Cancer, 5p, and Chief had already finished writing to it but were waiting on C-Lo's sixteen bars. They were all ready to record now, but C-Lo made it…knowing he wasn't on no lovey-dovey shit. So, 5P helped them record the song without Boss. In the song's title *Sex on Point,* Cancer wrote a fire hook:

"If my sex on point, would you be down for me/

Pick me up, take me out, would you clown with me/

Grab a fifth of a crown, would you drown with me/

56

All I really want to know is you down for me/. "

Every word in the hook was hurting C-Lo's heart. Didn't none of them know about Tiffany supposedly cheating with Bam; he just suffered through in silence. The song was past fire, but the end of 5P's verse is what really broke him down:

"Be around, be on my team/

put money in canteen/

is you gon' be down, or is you gon' go play around/

That's all I really want to know..."

Not only does it get to him, but it's striking and digging a deep hole within him. The end of 5P's verse was on repeat, replaying and echoing in his mind. *"Is you gon' be down, or is it you gon' play around, or is it you gon' play around, or is it you gon' play around... That's all I really want to know, want to know, want to know..."* The song sounded like a pure masterpiece.

***

"The Kop"

Hours later, way after the boys left, it was about time to start making moves. C-Lo went to his large bedroom and pulled out his money counter from the specialized spot he had installed on his floor.

After moving the tall green marble-colored dresser out of the way, he retrieved everything, including the bag with the $150,000 he picked up from Raven's crib earlier that day. He counted up $750,000 and some change. He wrapped bands around the stacks of $10,000 until he had $600,000, then put the money in two old Louis Vuitton bags. After The Kop, about $150,000 left, not counting their bank accounts and their pocket change.

He was set and had already given the green light to his BMClique to crank up from New Carter Apartments. If anything were to go wrong, he would go from almost becoming a millionaire to basically broke in his eyes.

Before he bounced, he told Tiffany harshly, "We need to talk when I get back."

"Yes, I have to talk to you too, baby," she replied.

"Just be careful. That's all that really matters."

"If I were to lose you, I don't know what I would do."

"Yes, cause I pay all the bills, bih!" he thought, but instead responded nonchalantly, "Yes, okay..."

She began to twist her face but instead said, "I love you!" She waited, hoping his response would be the same.

C-Lo turned, grabbed his Glock seventeen with an extra clip, and barked carelessly into the air, "Yea, I'll be back!" He walked out the door.

He didn't want to and couldn't get into it with her; it was too much work in the house to get into a heated quarrel only for her to call the police. As tipsy as he was, he had enough trouble, so he kept his mind clear. This was gone be a big kop; he couldn't be playing and not have his head screwed on tight. Tonight, could turn out to be the most important night of his entire life.

fifteen minutes later, he pulled back up and parked in the back of Empire off 8th Ave. 7th Ave was already getting thick, looking identical to the real New Orleans Mardi Gras, but this

58

was the way Ybor looked every weekend. He called Santana before he stepped out of his car and said, "I'm here."

"Just come to the side door. Somebody will let you in," Santana replied.

By the time he reached the door, he could see two of Santana's men at the door. One of the huge Hispanic men's names tags read: "Sergio." He followed him to Santana's office.

As he followed him up the swirl stairs, then around a sharp corner, you could see Santana and his brother Rico through a tall glass window next to a door that read: "Office". He entered to find himself sandwiched between the same two prominent Puerto Ricans sitting at the tables next to him when they all met earlier.

"Do you have the guns on you?" the bigger one asked who had reminded him of The Rock.

"Duh! With it rather than without it!" C-Lo replied as he reached for his ratchet. Both of the goons jumped back nervously, pulling their guns.

"Slow down, big fellows!" C-Lo pleaded, continuing slowly, and gave them his steel. They patted him down then used a metal detector wand on him and his bag.

One bobbed his head towards Rico. Santana offered a seat to C-Lo but he declined, "I'll stand!" He dropped the Louie bag on the desk in front of Rico. Santana, seated off in a chair to the side, opened the bag as Rico looked at C-Lo with a blank look.

"How much there?" Rico asked.

"What you mean! That check! Where's the shit?"

Rico bobbed his head towards his smaller goon, then motioned him towards two door that looked every bit like a closet. The bigger Puerto Rican came out with two large black leather bags and sat next to the money. Santana was stacking up on his desk. C-Lo slightly bobbed his head like he was listening to a low beat playing inside his brain, cracking a smile when Rico pulled out a key of cocaine.

"It's all here!" Santana told his brother, referring to the money.

"Good!" Rico finally spoke. He then grabbed a spoon and began a test called purification on the white girl for C-Lo. "This, my friend, is the best cocaine ya states have ever seen. This here is pure Ruby Pink straight from my country." C-Lo looked at the tube, and you could see the glint in his eyes as the solution turned dark purple. He knew the darker the berry, the deeper the roots. Meaning the darker it is, the stronger the juice, and the tube looked black. "You will find nothing in your country as pure."

C-Lo nudged his head, blocking out the rest of what he said, and grabbed the oversized bag. Rico continued, "From here on out, you'll be dealing with our cousin Castro! Just give him the rest of what you owe us, and as long as you come to get it, we will make them 10 apiece from here on out. Don't fuck us over, and we will keep you with whatever you need."

"Bet that up, Amigo! I gotcha!" C-Lo replied.

The Rock, which was the bigger one out of the Puerto Ricans, gave him his Glock when he exited. When he got to his car, he popped his trunk to his whip with his 'C' shaped diamond key chain, dropped all the work in, and closed the trunk. He looked around one time then got in the car. He smirked knowing that he was now one of the biggest, if not the biggest, in the city.

Jeezy: *"She likes (x3)! I'm a T.RA.P.S.T.A.R.!!!"*

Chapter 9

"VALUABLE LESSON"

C-Lo's headed back towards his house. It was about that time to meet up with Capone, so he gave him a holla! Capone picks up the phone while Dominique, the sexy young bartender, sits his ice and cranberry down in front of him.

"What's good, Lo?"

"Bout to be that way in a few, I just got to make one mo' stop," C-Lo replied.

"You aight! Handle that!"

"Aight! I'll be there in a few," C-Lo said.

"I'll see ya when you touchdown."

"Aight, superb fool," C-Lo responded jokingly.

"Yea, Yea!"

C-Lo hung up with quickness after seeing a police cruiser passing him, thinking he was about to get pulled over, he slipped on his Bluetooth because right now wasn't the time to get pulled over for a dumb-ass ticket like talking on the phone while driving. He didn't talk on his cell while driving, not without his Bluetooth in any way. Especially when he was riding dirty, and right now wasn't a good time to start.

Them crackers get crazy in Tampa, especially in Temple Terrace, and with just over a couple of million dollars' worth of drugs in the trunk…now wasn't a good time to test them. When he got to the house, Tiffany was sitting up watching Cheaters on TV.

"C-Lo… I'm so sick of being lonely, sitting here waiting by the phone. How did everything go?" she said.

"It went down. I need you to do me a favor," he replied.

"What's that, baby?" she asked.

"Go get one of my Lil Gucci bags out the studio while I put these things in the spot."

He was about to give Capone the last seven bricks he had left from his latest batch. He was tried and a little tipsy from earlier still and just wanted to get him out of his hair. The fresh one hundred blocks needed cooking ASAP, so tomorrow was the perfect time to get Snapp and Yoda Boy on the first twenty-five. He went and put up seventy-five bricks in the spot, with the bag that held the other twenty-five and sat them neatly on his floor wide safe, while Tiffany brought him the bag, he was to fill with the old work he just emptied out of the safe.

As she walked out of the bedroom, she asked nicely, "I'm finished cooking! You want me to make you a plate?"

"What you fixed?" he asked.

"Sirloin steak, Diane-in-chive sauce, with sliced buttered potatoes with rolls, and…"

"Just fix me one of those fire steak sandwiches!" he said, cutting her off.

When he tightened everything up, he went downstairs carrying his Gucci bag across his shoulder filled to the rim. When he walked in the kitchen, she had his sandwich made up as he loved it, with the melted cheese. He snatched a grape soda out of the cooler and his Gucci bag he'd sat down, threw it over his shoulder, and headed towards the front door to leave.

"Umm, we gone talk when you get back or what?" Tiffany asked, sounding frustrated.

He studied her for a split second and replied, "Yea, we gone talk!" He walked out and closed the door.

Besides their minor Bam-Bam issue, she needed to tell him that she was pregnant and doesn't know if he's the father or not, but that she planned on keeping it no matter what. Well, probably not all of that. Just the idea of it not being his child troubled her, but he deserved the truth, and the truth should have been told to him when she found out the other day. "The truth shall set you free!" she tried to convince herself. But the truth didn't usually set people free. It just made them crazier. Most people can't handle the truth.

"I found ya missing ring that you left at Bam-Bam's place! Oh yeah, and by the way, you can kick rocks, bih!" C-Lo played in his head as he headed towards Apollo South. He knew he needed to tell her. He still loved her, but she brought the wrath he was about to release upon herself.

***

"Birthday Bash"

The Apollo was thick as always and even thicker because it was Kebo's Birthday Bash, and he was popping bottles after bottles. Food lined the whole wall, and drinks were free after midnight for everybody. Dj Shiszm was on the ones and twos, and all the homeboys were there. Mike-Mike, Monsta, Boo-Boo, Hot-Rod, Yayo, Gutter, Junk, Fat-Boy, Charlie, Junkie, Bump, Rick, Cal, Sexy, Zoe, T-Money, and LaBron Chevy two-four and even Bernard and Cago were buying up the bar.

Capone was at a small table on the side stage, sitting next to his boy forty, but by himself. C-Lo went over and had a seat. They made a little small talk but mostly talked about Bam's death. They still couldn't put together who or why anybody would put that steel to him. Niggas know exactly who BMC was.

It was time for the business at hand.

"You play pool?" C-Lo asked Capone.

"One of the best who've done it."

"Well, let's run one while we finish talking!"

They headed over to the pool table to rack the balls. C-Lo had something up his sleeve.

"Let's make a friendly wager?" C-Lo offered.

"You don't want to lose ya money, Lo!"

He laughed, "I got seven of the things in the car. Ya, hear me! If you lose, you buy them tonight for 15 stacks apiece. If you win, I'll front them to you for 12 stacks apiece, even though the price is 17 from here on out. It's a win-win situation! You with it?"

Capone answered with quickness, "Damn right! The question is, are you ready for this!"

"Most definitely! I was born ready!" C-Lo replied devilishly.

"Yea, OK! Finish racking them balls! That's what they all say. All I want to know is who gone break?" Capone asked.

"Let's flip for it. Heads I break, tails you break."

Capone replied, "Aight!"

C-Lo did the toss and won, "Let's use the 8-ball to break instead of the Cue-ball and place the Cue-ball in the middle of the rack where the eight-ball should be."

Capone looked perplexed and puzzled. "So, we gone substitute the eight-ball with the cue-ball?" he asked.

C-Lo jokingly answered, "That's right, and I want to show you a thing-a-ma-jig or two."

It was a valuable lesson to be learned for both of them; one of the reasons was to find out where Capone's head was. Capone passed him the blunt he was smoking while C-Lo twisted together his pool stick, getting ready to break. After a few pulls and finishing putting his post together, he broke the eight-ball, and two solid balls fell. He then pulled on the sweet-smelling dro and murmured while he was shooting his next shot.

"You know the history behind this game?" C-Lo asked.

"What do you mean?"

C-Lo sighed, upset, rudely saying, "three-ball side pocket!" He took a hard pull of the blunt, handed it to Capone, and inhaled deeply, releasing all the smoke through the air before he knocked in the three-ball. As he chalked up the tip of his stick, he bent over to observe his next shot. "Knowledge is to be looked for, not just given. Well, that's what the face Mason's believe, true or not. That's why they created the game... five-ball corner pocket!" He hit the eight-ball, it connected to the orange ball and dropped. At the same time, he surveyed the eight-ball that got away down the green too far to set up his next shot.

C-Lo reached for the blunt and asked, "What color is the table?"

"Green!" Capone returned, lost while he pulled the weed.

"OK, that represents the earth itself. It's six holes. The earth is round, not flat, right?" "Yea! So, you get it, now?"

"The table's the earth! The world is round! What's the point?" Capone asked.

C-Lo again pulled the blunt, creating a heavy mist, "What's the object of the game?"

Capone answered, "To knock all the balls off the table, then the eight-ball."

"No! Wrong!" C-Lo corrected him, chalking up his stick again, giving the blunt another hard pull before he dropped the roach, stepped on it, and took his next shot, trying to keep every bit of smoke in.

The eight-ball jumped clearly over a strip ball and tipped the two-ball into the side pocket. He smiled. "The game's objective is for the white ball to knock off all the nationalities from the world, one by one. Hold up, hold up, hold up…seven-ball cross the corner pocket off the one-ball," C-Lo continued and hit the eight-ball gracefully; it hits his shot just how he called it. Then for a second, studied the table, "one-ball, two times, back down here to the left corner pocket." He sets up his shot, closed one eye, opened it, then stroked his stick with confidence. The yellow ball went around the table, came back dragging, and stopped, then fell in the hole C-Lo called.

"Where was I?" C-Lo stood up and stared Capone directly into his eyes and continued. "Oh, yea! After the white ball, which represents the White Man, knocks off all the different colors, all races, and nationalities, right? Then the White man knocks, my bad, kills off who last?"

"The Blackball!" Capone responds.

"That's right! Which are Black Men. So, now you get it? But this time who is the last man standing...cue-ball corner pocket." He pointed to the pocket he called, bent over, lined up his shot, then stroked his stick to hit the 8-ball. The 8-ball made a spiral move around the 10-ball, rolled down the green, hit the cue-ball, went straight to the hole he called, and dropped. C-Lo picked up the 8-ball and showed him the only man standing. "The thing is, we have to be much brighter than the next man so that we can be the last ball standing."

He replaced the ball, dropping it inside the side pocket, symbolizing that even the last man standing someday must die. "But this game doesn't last forever, bruh! This dope game is very much the same way, but what we live in is far from a game. It is our life as we know it! Now, these mothafucka's got us killing off ourselves. Just like Bam-Bam, they'll knock us off and leave us dead as a doorknob, but only if we don't take control of everything around us and become more intelligent. It is our faith! It is reality!"

Capone smiled at him while he untwisted his pool stick because he had just taught him two valuable lessons in one that nobody in his life ever took the time to teach him. For one, never leave home without it, and two, be the first to shoot.

They both agreed to meet up tomorrow so he could drop C-Lo that cash, but he still gave him that work.

***

"Many Men"

After chilling a bit longer in the parking lot with some of the homies, it was time for C-Lo to bust some moves, feelings his eyes become heavy. When he left, he made a U-turn to come back up 40th, flying past Apollo Lounge with only one thing in mind, his king-sized bed.

He stopped at the red light on 40th and Hillsborough and slightly closed his eyes. Still feeling a little tipsy, without dozing off, mentally calm, he saw Disarray's face. He was picturing himself scorched by Co and TJ to finish her off. He was holding a gun between her eyes. It was that full moon night in that warehouse where they deviously tortured and killed the three people. As C-Lo pulled the trigger, creating the final glow from the blast that killed her, he jumped out of his trance and saw the traffic light was green. Cars behind him started honking.

"Come on, man, don't you see the light green!"

"Wake-up nigga damn!"

Meanwhile, Dang sat in Gyros drive-thru off of 40th and Hillsborough, getting some food, when he heard yelling and horns blowing at C-Lo's Red Benz as it was rolling past the intersection flying by Gyro's. "Oh shit! Der go that fuck nigga right der!" Dang barked out loud to himself. He pulled off hastily, forgetting his order he was so in a rush.

C-Lo didn't need to make any more stops tonight, but he never went straight to the house, in case somebody was ever following him. He saw headlights from a smaller black car and circled his block twice. After investigating behind him in the rear-view mirror, not finding a vehicle in sight, he safely headed to the house, still listening to his radio. *"They got me staring at the world through my rear-view/ baby you can scream to God he can hear you."*

He parked in his driveway, grabbed his extra clip pouch out of the glove-box and turned and grabbed his laptop bag out of his backseat. He finished getting his things together, got out, slid his Glock 17 in his waistband, then retrieved his laptop bag out of his driver seat. He proceeded to walk around his car as he hit the car alarm remote and fumbled over his hand full of keys, looking for his front door key when he heard something. Out of nowhere, a dark gunman appeared in his presence. The masked man's voice was stern but clear.

"What's up nigga!"

C-Lo never had a chance to grab his Glock 17 from his waist. *Pow pow pow pow!* Four shots from the masked gunman. One hit C-Lo in the hip bone, another in his left upper leg area, and another in his left arm. He dropped his keys as he followed them to the ground, feeling a fiery sensation. The shadow stepped in the way of the street light hovering over C-Lo's helpless body to finish him off. Dang yelled something as he pulled the trigger to his lord and tried to continue to let off shots to kill C-Lo. But he couldn't focus due to the screaming sound coming from the house; it was Tiffany.

She flung the front door open and Dang fled the scene. This time it didn't feel like Deja Vu. It was Déjà because it was exactly like his dream that morning…but this time it was very much real.

"Many men! Many, many, many, many men! Wish death on me. Dawg, I don't cry anymore, don't look to the sky anymore! Have mercy on many men Pow!"

Chapter 10

"MIRANDA!"

The next day C-Lo woke up sore with Tiffany sitting by his side. "Charles! Charles! Wake up, C-Lo! Come on, baby, you got to eat something!"

They were in the hospital, last night was far from a dream. After being shot five times, he'd been hospitalized and had to go through emergence surgery to remove two out of five bullets that hit him. Lucky wasn't the word, blessed to be alive is what it was, but not lucky enough not to be handcuffed to a hospital bed.

"What the hell!" C-Lo dramatically yanked his cuffed hand like he could remove himself. After seeing it wasn't budging, he settled on lifting it in the air, demanding an explanation. Tiffany explained that he was under arrest, and the cops were charging him with a felony in possession of a firearm. "When you came to the hospital, they called the police, not just because of the gunshot wounds, but because the staff, or maybe the Paramedics, found the gun on your waist."

"Bullshit! A motherfucker tryna kill me in my fuckin front yard, and I got to go to jail! What kind of fuck ass shit is that!"

"Calm down, baby. I thought you was dead when I heard the shot then found you laying in the doorway in all that blood."

"What! What the fuck you mean, calm down! What kind of shit you on! A bih just shot me! I see you remember that...but do you not understand that!"

He was so loud, the cop standing guard outside of his room came in and he hadn't noticed. "Good morning Mr. Jones! Do we have a problem?"

"Problem! Hell no! Besides being chained to a fuckin hospital bed like a wild animal, I'm doing great, Officer. Not a problem in the world!" C-Lo said sarcastically.

"Good. A few detectives are on their way up to ask you a couple of questions concerning last night. I just wanted to advise you of your Miranda Rights."

After he advised him of his rights and remained silent, the Officer asked him if he had any questions.

"I don't want to sound dumb or turn this into 21 questions, but what's the reason I was put under arrest?"

"Possession of a concealed firearm, Sir." After the detectives speak with you and the hospital releases you, you'll be sent to Orient Road and booked and given a bond."

C-Lo just dropped his head in pitifulness and couldn't say another word. His body was in so much pain he looked around for some pain medication. He laid back down without hope and closed his eyelids until the Officer exited smoothly without making a sound.

He told Tiffany he needed her more than ever before. "Call my lawyer and bond me out as soon as I get booked in!" He started to tell her the safe combo but instead told her to call Capone to get what he owes me. That's way more than enough to bond me out and pay the lawyer if needed.

While they conversed, the two detectives walked in unannounced. They looked identical to the Blues Brothers. One kind of like Jim Blushe, but the 2nd one was tall sharp with a Cuban cigar hanging from the corner of his mouth. You could tell he wasn't a rookie by a long Degree. C-Lo was ready for their good cop bad cop routine as the taller 2nd man spoke first.

"How you feeling, Mr. Jones?"

"How the fuck you think I'm feeling!" a motherfucker shot me and left me for dead on my front lawn, and I'm about to go to jail! You tell me how I suppose to feel!" he lost it!

"Sir, we know how you...."

"Hold up, hold up! Who the fuck is WE, anyways? The CIA, ATF, the FBI. Home Security or some shit?" C-Lo chuckled while the shorter officer went to speak again, not finding his comment a bit amusing.

"Sir, we know how you feel."

"Buddy! You don't know how I feel! You wouldn't know where to begin!!! You know how I feel!"

"Calm down, Sir!"

"Calm down? Psshhh, there you go."

"Please, Sir, Calm down. Let me start over. My name is Det. Brown, and this here is my partner Det. Moore. We're trying to do everything, everything in our power to find out who shot you and why." Det. Brown looked over at Tiffany, "I'm sorry, Ms. Lady. Can you please exit the room so we can ask Charles a few questions?" She gave both of them an evil look like they were one of the dudes who shot and hospitalized her man. As she strolled out the room, she stared them both down.

"Sorry for the inconvenience, Sir, but we only have a few questions for you, Mr. Jones. First of all, do you know who shot you or have any idea who?"

He spared a dumb look at Det. Moore and his partner and answered back like a true white boy. "No, Sir, I don't know who shot me!"

"We need to know what happened. Can you tell us?"

"Yea, last night I was getting home from my homeboy's birthday party when I pulled up to my house and got out of my car. Somebody put a few caps in my ass! I thought y'all was the fuckin police! Y'all sho' ask some dumb ass questions!" C-Lo sucked his teeth, becoming frustrated.

"Well, Sir, we don't know what happened! That's what we're trying to figure out!" Det. Brown responded.

Det. Moore interrupted, "Yea, it's not every day people get shot for nothing! We believe it's somebody you know. These days it's usually a dope boy robbery or a drug deal gone bad! Do you sell drugs, Mr. Jones?"

"Naw! Y'all tripping! What fucking kind of question is that?"

"It's just a question, Sir. Let me ask you this then. Do you know anybody whatsoever who might want you dead, you or your friend Bam-Bam?" That had caught C-Lo off guard, but that was a good question. One he wasn't ready for, but one he needed to ask himself.

"No, I don't know, but I know y'all motherfuckers need to get off y'all Cuban cigar-smoking, doughnut-eating fat asses up and find these bitches made Inga's that's out there. Trying ta kill all us off and shit!"

Det. Moore bites down on his cigar, "Sir, we can't help you if you don't help us, and we know you know something about Bam's death...way more than you are trying to lead us to believe, but we haven't put it together yet!"

The thing is, the police didn't know any more than he did, and he really couldn't help them out at all about anything, even if he wanted to. He hadn't put the clues together and was just as lost as they were. "I don't know shit bout nothing, bout it, or who, and if I did know, you would be the first to find out cause they'd be dead already."

Detective Brown rubbed his temple shaking his head, "Don't take nothing into your own hands. That will be the wrong thing to do. Here's my number..."

"Ah! 9-1-1 is a joke!" C-Lo mumbled under his breath.

"C-Lo, if you want to talk, or remember anything, call either of us at either number."

He took the cards, and they left. As soon as the door shut, he flicked the card towards the door, "That's why I don't like cops! We hold court in the streets wherein from. I'm a street nigga. I'm allergic to black and blue!" He then lifted his head to the ceiling. "Dear God, thanks for looking after me and sparing my life again. Without you, Lord, I'm nothin'! Without ya hands on my life, I would have been dead. Thank you, Father!"

It was no guessing he knew what he was referencing. He tried to recite the 23rd Psalm but only could remember verse 4, "Even though I walk through the valley of the shadow of death, I will fear no evil, for you are with me."

Chapter 11

"ORIENT RD"

Later that night, C-Lo was transferred to Orient Road Jail. The whole day after the shooting, Capone tried to hit him but couldn't reach him on his cell phone. He tried all day continuously with no luck until Tiffany called him.

"Hello?" Capone answered.

"Hey."

"Hey, Sexy!"

"Is this Capone?"

"Hell yeah! Who dis?"

"This Tiffany! C-Lo's wife! He told me to call you."

"O shit, my bad! I didn't know it was you; I've been trying to reach him all day. What's wrong with his phone?"

"C-Lo got shot last night after leaving the bar," she said.

"What! What happened? He aight?"

"He got shot five times right in front of the house! The doctors or the paramedics found his Glock on his hip trying to save his life! He told me he needs for you to go post his bond."

"Bond!" he repeated loudly.

"Yea! He's in jail! That's what I have been trying to tell you! Can you meet me in like thirty minutes at John's bail bondman's office on Orient Road? It's right across the street from the jail with what you owe him."

"Yea, I'm on my way!"

He had just jumped out some twat, so he had to tighten up a few loose ends and called her back shortly after. He told her to meet him there in another twenty minutes. C-Lo's bond was $20,000, but the whole thing wasn't a problem for Capone if need be. When he got there, she already had the paperwork finished. He paid John's secretary out of his pocket, and she told them, "Charles should be out in about twenty-four hours, depending on however long it takes the jail to process and finish booking him."

Capone walked Tiffany to her car and popped her trunk so that he could drop the two nice size Gucci bags in it. "Look, I got to change some lanes, but the buck-o-five I owe him is in his Gucci bag, I put in your truck. Tell fool I said hit me ASAP, I mean soon as he jumps, no if and or buts. It doesn't matter what time that be, Okay?" Capone said.

"I'll tell 'em."

Due to all the madness taking place, C-Lo didn't trust a soul, but he also figured that if Capone had anything to do with his hit, he would at least wait til he had some of the bricks on him first. Plus, he had eight bands in his pocket. He still had every penny when he awakened in the hospital, plus all his jewels.

So, it was far from a robbery. That made him realize the person who touched him was only trying to kill him. So, it wasn't business…it was business. Whoever shot them had something coming, he put that on his dead grandmother's head. "Fuck business!" It had turned personal.

***

"It Couldn't Be"

After they posted C-Lo's bond, Tiffany figured she had a few hours before they'd release him. She remembered her ring wasn't on her finger again. She didn't take it lightly. It wasn't just an ordinary ring; it was her engagement rock. Her mind began racing. "When was the last time I've seen it? Bam's house! No! It could be!"

She shot home first, no further than twenty minutes from the jail. When she finally got there, she searched high and low. She tore up every possible spot and had only one clue on where she left it. "Bam's house! It couldn't be!" She thought about calling Coco but her and Lil Man were probably sound asleep already. Plus, she never worked on Saturdays. She sat on her bed's red satin sheets and tried to brainstorm, rubbing her fingers through her crinkly hair.

"It had to be only missing about a day or so…Okay I think I had it on yesterday. I never take it off, but for two reasons. One to do dishes and two to do work in my garden, or… ohhh my God, when I suck my man up!" She paused. "Damn!" That thought reassured her that she likely left it at Bam's place. "Naw! It couldn't be!" The thought turned her into a nervous wreck to the point she lost track of time searching. It was getting super late and C-Lo would be getting released very soon. So, she left heading back to the jail, knowing it would only be a nick of time before he started questioning her about her naked finger.

When she arrived back at the jail, she checked with the fat front desk clerk, but was only told not yet. She sat in the parking lot in her freshly painted pink and purple old legend sitting on 22's and fell asleep. She was awakened shortly after dozing off from someone tapping on her driver's window. She jumped up, spooked out of her sleep.

"Baby?" C-Lo had just been released. He had a sling on his left arm, with all his property in a cheap plastic bag hopping on a crutch. She automatically unlocked the doors so he could leap in. It was close to 3 in the morning.

"Did you call Capone?" he asked.

"I love you too!" she replied. "Yes! I did! He gave me what he owed you, plus bonded you out. He told me to tell you to hit 'em up soon as you got out."

"Where the bags?"

"Ya Guccis are in da trunk, and no I haven't opened them!"

"Stop by the store so I can get me some Jewel sweets," he said.

They stopped at the gas station, then McDonald's to get a bite to eat, then took it in for the night. When they got home, he didn't call Capone. He had a list of people to call when he woke up, so he added him to the list. As soon as he lay down his eyes got heavy. While Tiffany wrapped his arms around her, before he dozed off. He contemplated if he wanted to confront her about her engagement ring he found and that he knew she was cheating on him, but decided to wait.

She turned towards him, pondering telling him about her ring before she fully dozed off. "Oh, yeah! What I suppose to tell

79

him? I think I lost my engagement ring at your best friend place…It couldn't be!" She paused her hypothetical confession. "And it's probably when I took it off, to get him off. And, oh yeah…I'm pregnant and it might not be yours, but your dead best friend's…. Damn! It couldn't be!" What if the baby was Bam's? What if this wasn't C-Lo's? "It couldn't be!" She knew he'd never live if down or let her… "Better yet, would he kick my ass and or kick my ass out on the streets?" She wanted to figure out who the father was before telling him, she wanted to be sure.

She cuddled closer in his arms, "Damn, I dun fucked up! I'll get rid of this lil bastard before I tell 'em it's Bam Bam's baby," she thought to herself, before dozing off peacefully to sleep next to C-Lo.

Chapter 12

"AFTERMATH"

The following morning Tiffany was up before C-Lo and was about to finish cooking Sunday's breakfast.

"Earlier one Sunday morning... Breakfast was on the table. There was no time to eat, and she said to me, boy, hurry for Sunday School...."

Bright and early his phone commences to buzz off the hook. The first person trying to link up with him was Capone. C-Lo rolled over and yawned from the aftermath. While answering his iPhone, "Hello!"

"What it be like?"

"I'm Gucci fool! I got that package blood. Thanks for coming to bail a Nigga out, Bruh."

"Yeah, whatever! You gone tell me what happened or what!"

"Remember when I said a nigga will try and knock you off?"

"Yeah! How can I forget now?"

"You bet not! You see what I mean now. A bih tried to knock my head loose blood and left me fa dead fool!"

"That's some fuck shit, dawg! Did they get the squares?"

"Nah! They buried already."

"It don't matter, them nigga's might as well be dead already! Who you think the one behind it?"

"I don't know, really, but you know that nigga Phats?"

"Yeah, Big Dave! The fat boy he called Phat Cat in school."

"I think that nigga had something to do with it, but check it. I also think that the same person that killed Bam-Bam Shot me. The absurd part is, he don't have enough balls or heart to shoot me or at me. Let alone have enough nerve to kill a nigga period, or even try anyway!"

"Whoever it was, Lo, already signed their death certificate when we find out who did it!"

"Fool, when I find out who did it, they dead! I'm gone make sure of that myself, trust that!"

"If you need anything, dawg, I mean anything, just let me know. Real talk! I got them thangs like T.I… I'm ready for war over here and been this way since knee-high." Capone laughed and C-Lo joined in, laughing along with him, reciting a line from Shawty Lo's song, *They Know.*

"Well, I'm gone need ya to sho' then. I got a lil fire, but it's not even close to what I need to slow a nigga down. Not with what I plan for who shot me!"

"Man, I'm down with whatever. When you ready to do that, I can holla at my brother Desmond. He got some shit that will blow off Fort Knox doors!"

"Let's bring down the world trade center then!"

The call waiting beep on C-Lo's line. He peeped to see it was his brother and let Capone know he'd holla back!

"Hello!" C-Lo answered.

Chief and Cancer were on three-way, and they doubled-teamed C-Lo, "What the hell goin' on, Bruh? You straight over there?"

"Yea, a little sore, but I'm blessed to be alive, bruh."

"Damn right you are, but who the fuck was they?" Cancer asked hot-tempered.

"I don't know, Cuzzo. All I remember is, I was coming from the spot when I got home. I got out my car, walked toward my front door, then I heard a bih say something. Next thing I know, the motherfucker let loose on me, Cuzo. I could feel every inch of the steel melt through my flesh. Somebody trying to kill me, Bruh!"

Cancer responded, sounding lost, "And you still there! You need to get the fuck out of that house. Like ASAP! They know exactly where you lay your head, Bruh! You don't think they'll try and pop you again! Foreal foreal! You need to make that move ASAP and get the hell out of dodge!"

Not wanting to disagree with his little brother, he agreed to disagree. "Y'all might be right, but they might think I'm dead already."

Cancer checked that nonsense, "Fuck all that might be stuff. You not, and that not hard to find out at all, Boss."

"Bruh, you need to come stay with me til you can make that move!"

"Chief, first of all, you don't have that kinda room for me, Tiff, you, and ya baby mama... plus both y'all kids for even just one day."

"I was just gonna," Chief started.

"Naw, you don't! Second, if I was gonna leave, I'll just get a hotel or something. I'm gone get Tiff to stay with her sister for a while. I'll tell you this, though, and I'll be damn if I let a bih just run me away from home like I'm some type of bitch!" C-Lo said sternly.

"I feel you, but you have to watch niggas bruh. They just tried to kill you. Don't take ya life for granted!" Chief said.

Cancer agreed, "Right, fam, I basically just told you that! Tiff told us you got hit five times."

2-Pac: *"Busters shot me five times. Real niggas don't die. Can ya hear me? Laced with this game, I know you fear me...."*

"Shit, yea! It burnt like hell too. One grazed my hip, and another went through my left thigh and my arm. My leg was straight, but they had to remove two bullets, one out my chest and the other from my shoulder. It hurts like a bih! Bottom line God spared the kid for some reason."

Tiffany called upstairs. C-Lo's Mom had just pulled up in the driveway. He cut it short and told his peeps he was good and would call them because Mom Dukes had just got there.

"Okay, bruh, superb!" Chief said.

"Superb!"

"Aight Cuzzo, superb!" Cancer said.

"Superb, Lil fool!"

He poured some pain pills in his hand, overloading them in his mouth before downing them with a glass of warm water next to the bed. He grabbed his grandma's old wooden Cain and headed downstairs with a limp. The doorbell rang as he was starting down the steps, then again, causing Tiffany to react.

"I got it, baby!"

She met him at the front door, but he was already opening it. No one had told his Mom or his sister he'd been shot and put in jail. It was still early and his Mom was on her way to Church.

"Hey, baby boy! Oh, Man! What happened, son? What's wrong with yo arm? What's wrong with yo leg?" his mom, Mrs. Joyce, asked as she walked in.

"Oh, mama, you worry too much!"

"Don't I suppose to be concerned about my son's well-being? I wouldn't be a mother, well, a good one if I didn't!"

"I'm grown!"

"Yea, you grown, but you still my baby boy. You just my baby boy!"

"Hello, Mrs. JJ!" Tiffany greeted.

"Hey, Tiffany. What you did to the boy, na? Beat him up and pushed him down the stairs or something?"

"No, Mama! It wasn't me this time!" They both giggled softly.

"Would you like some breakfast or something to drink? I have some hot coffee?"

"No, baby."

"Freshly made!" Tiffany said.

"No, baby, I'm fine. Thanks!" she turned to her son. "I just stopped by to tell you I'm on the way to get your kids for Church. Have you talked to that crazy lady?"

"Who, Pinky?" C-Lo replied.

***

"Family Ties!"

Pinky is his babymama; her real name is Devilisha. She's a sexy Amazon standing at six foot one and two hundred and five pounds. Her body is so perfectly round it's a shame. She's gorgeous as hell and hell on wheels, all in the same swing. Forty-six double D's, and with her thick frame, there's no question she could be a plus-size model. As a matter of fact, she could be Toccara's twin. Yes sir, a true BBW.

She was from Suphur Springs, one of T-Town's roughest neighborhoods, if not the toughest hood. Everybody knew her and her two brother's Rayfield and Carl, because they were Drak Boyz. She also had a half-brother by the name of Kequon, better known as K.B., from the West. C-Lo grew up with him, not knowing their relationship at the time. C-Lo met her while chilling playing basketball one weekend at Giddens Park in Dirty Game, where he grew up. It felt like a match made in heaven when they first met. She was on the swings looking sad, hopelessly heartsick; he couldn't stand it when he saw her spiritless.

In between games, he sat out to make her smile. He went and jumped on the swing open next to her, then acted as if he was about to fall backwards while swinging as high as possible.

"If you fall, I'm gone laugh at you!" Devilisha had told him.

"Damn! You gone laugh at me? That's not nice. You gone see if I'm aight first?" C-Lo asked.

"Yea! I'll see if you okay, then I'm gone laugh at you!"

They laughed, talked, and got to know each other from that point on. They were very young and only a year apart. They did everything together and went everywhere together and the sex…was amazing. But they started having problems four months into the sexually based relationship. They couldn't stop arguing over dumb, unnecessary stuff. He finally worked up the nerve to leave her. He thought it was best they both go their separate ways. When he broke it off, she stormed out the front door raising all types of hell. "Yes, Lawd! I'm done with her forever!" he remembered thinking, even though it did hurt him. Before she left, she turned around and told him news that let him know he spoke to fast.

"Oh yeah! I'm pregnant, you dumb fuck!" she said, slamming the door again all in one motion.

He breathed in and muttered, "Damn, I'm gone have to put up with this crazy chick forever now!"

He had grown attached to her and had deep feelings for her. He set out to make it work and tried to mold them into that family he always wanted. You know the family that had both parents in the house, nice job, two cars, the big house with the white picket fence. He wanted to raise his kids. He knew he could teach them more than anybody else on the face of the earth would. So, they ended up getting back together, and a little under a year later their first child was born, Charlizia, a healthy baby girl.

Pinky and C-Lo gave it another shot moving back in together. Times were good. Sex was great, but that always could be a trap to keep a good brother. The same thing in this case, but they were back fighting too much. They'd fight then turn around and have make-up sex. Fight again then make-up sex. Somewhere between all the arguing and then fighting, plus good sex, Pinky ended up pregnant again. This time with their baby boy, C.J. (Charles Jr). His nickname was Lil Serious, born a year after Charlizia. It was good for a while, but it was a wrap shortly after Lil Serious was born. It was worse than ever before.

"I talk to Charlie and Lil Serious all the time. You didn't know I got them both phones a couple of months back?" C-Lo told him mom. He didn't deal with his baby mother at all in any way. Mostly because she'd acted a fool on him any and everywhere, way too many times. Her name said it all, Devilisha! "Can you drop them off after Church? I'll take 'em home!" He hadn't seen them in weeks, just because they couldn't communicate, but it was only hurting the kids.

"I'll call you when we get out of church," his mother said and left.

C-Lo decided it was time to call this new lawyer that his homeboy talked so highly of, but he didn't get a chance to before his phone ring again. *"I run dis bitch! I'm gon keep running, but I'm never running out of money! I'm a..."* It was Gator.

"Hey, what's good, G?"

"I'm good! How you feeling C-Lo?"

"Okay. What's the problem?"

"My close friend Bobby."

"Cool?"

"He got shot."

"Him too?! My bad! He aight?"

"Lo. He got hit with a stick seventeen times the night before last."

"Damn! Seventeen times! That was the night I got hit!"

"Yea, I know. It got me stuck wondering who wanted Cool dead so bad! I just wish I knew."

"I bet you do! So, what you gone do?"

"Well, the funeral is in three days. I want to head down that way and show my respect. If you feeling up to it, I want to know if you'll drive down there with me?"

"Yea!!! You want me to drive, don't you?"

"Please! Only if your leg feels alright. I go to court about my L's next month...."

"Say no more! I'll do that for you. Damn seventeen times tho? I can't do anything but imagine. That's a lot of hate and damn sho a lot of bullets for one man."

"We'll see what went down when we get down there."

"You might not want to! But aight! Let me finish doing what I was doing. I'll bark back at ya."

"Yeah, okay. Tell my girl I said I love her."

"Ten four, Pops!"

When C-Lo hung up, he figured he had plenty of time to call his lawyer, so instead, he called Meatball and Rex to see what was up with the apartments over on the east side. Ball let him know he needs to make his way that way to help finish organizing the operation. C-Lo let them know he had the blueprint mapped out already, and he'd holla back at him to get them right in a little bit. He was trying to delay, getting some of that work whipped up.

After numerous calls to different members of the BMClique, he knew project "Carter" had to be his priority because nobody wanted any real work. He geared his mind up to focus on that significant move, but the first thing was first. He called Snapp and Big Yoda Boy to get them started on baking up the first twenty-five bricks.

Before he could hang up good from Yoda Boy, Tiffany yelled, "Ohh-wee! Who this outside in my car!" He stood up, looking outside the living room window to see his girl's dream car alright. The same one she wants him to buy her, parked right outside in their driveway. It was a black Excursion with tinted windows and had a chromed-out lining sitting on twenty-six-inch Rims.

C-Lo grabbed his old 38, put it in the back of his waistband, and retrieved his basketball from behind the door. He took a few steps outside the door and started dribbling the ball. A few seconds later, the driver window went down automatically. It seemed screen by screen in slow motion. He cuffed the ball and clutched his fire. When the window passed the driver's nose, you knew who it was, Big E!

"If I don't get you straight today, Man, I'll get you straight tomorrow! Big Old E told me we'd be okay tomorrow! Tomorrow! Tomorrow! Tomorrow! Yeah!"

"What's up, baby boy!"

"What's up? You almost got popped! That's what's sup blood!"

"Yea! Almost ain't close enough B! What you know bout that rack, doe?" E was referring to the basketball C-Lo was holding.

"Bruh, out of all the people you know, I hold my own like A.I. baby! What's hood doe fool?"

"Nothing! I was in the neighborhood, so I just stopped thinking."

"New! To see a little fish like me in the big lo pond!"

"Yeah nigga!" Big E responded to C-Lo's sarcastic remake.

"That's what's good but check it. You got to come to our show at One Twelve next week. Plus, we bout finish with the album!"

"How does it sound?" Big E asked.

"I can show you better than I can tell ya."

He takes E in the studio and played a bunch of jams off the most anticipated L.P. "Grindin Season" and a handful of new beats coming out of BloodMoney Records.

Big E bobbed his head in excitement, "Man C... Keep doin ya thang man! You got a niche for this music shit! Too real, you know what you doin! Plus, listen to yo beats! They banging! They harder than the best in the game right na. Dre's, Pharelle, Cool & Dre, Kanye West, all of them!"

As they continued to talk, C-Lo saw something bothering his big homie. "Yea, but what's hood doe, E? Looks like something eating you up! You aight fool?"

"Don't worry ya self with my problems, young breed!"

"Whatever! You know yo beef is my beef fool! So, what's hood?"

"Man, C...I don't want to get you mixed up in the bullshit..."

"Man, what happened, nigga? Damn!"

"Some motherfuckers robbed me dawg, for thirty-five large!" Big E said, paused then continued, "and I think it was all over some hoe shit!" He pulled out a black and Chrome 9mm, with a pretty black gray grip, and cocked it back as he finished,"And I'll be dammed if they rob me again!"

C-Lo pictured how he'd killed Daz'aray in cold blood and how it always haunted him. Big E had that same look in his eyes now, the face of a killer.

"Sometimes it's not always about getting even. It's 'bout living to fight that next fight and seeing another day," C-Lo said.

"Yea, I know, kid. If you let a bitch take from you, C, they might feel they can always take from you, and I ain't on that! I'll be damn it they rob me again! That's what God Love yo!"

They talked and vibed for a good little while before he took flight, C-Lo was worried about his mentor, but he couldn't be because he was a big boy in this big world, with big money, with big toys and kept a big ole toy!! He went in the house to relax for the rest of the day after they broke off to watch the NBA Finals.

When his kids got there, the house got nosier; both of them were adorable. They looked as if he spit 'em out himself. Cj, being a boy, not only was a still image of him, he was just like him. Besides that, he was so serious all the time. Charlizia on the other hand, was a female portrait and a daddy's girl, and so pretty. She wouldn't let him walk from one room to the other attached firmly to his hip. You know without a doubt that she was his child. Her mother Pinky once asked her who she loved the most! "Daddy," Charlie told her Mother, "My Daddy!" Pinky slapped fire from the little girl for answering a question with honesty.

"I'm your mother you dumb ass little girl," Pinky had told her then turned toward Lil Serious without saying a word. He caught on quick, saying, "You Mommy! I love you more, mommy!" What Pinky failed to realize was that you don't ask kids that kind of question or make a child choose between their parents. For one, you might not want their honest answer, and two, you just don't put them in those kinds of situations, and you don't treat kids that way.

It didn't matter how much he grew to dislike their mother when it came to his kids. He'd loved them with all his heart and soul. He wouldn't change or regret meeting Devilisha for nothing in the world.

"I love ya, Daddy!"

"I love ya to, Charlie!"

"I love you, Daddddddyyyyyy!!!"

"I love you too, Serious!"

Chapter 13

"READY FOR WAR"

Monday came around, and C-Lo talked to his lawyer, Mrs. Kelly. She informed him she was only charging him five thousand dollars but gave him no promises what would happen. He also got in contact with Capone.

"What's good, Lo?"

"You know! I need you to call ya, brother. I'm bout to drop some bread in his lap!"

"I'll hit you back with the business in a second."

"Bet that up, fool!"

He hit his brother Dezmond up, who went by Big Dez. People thought they were twins, but realistically, they were almost five years apart. Dez wasn't the one to touch any type of drugs. Didn't drink and hardly smoked weed. For one, so his gun import would never get hot, and so he wouldn't get messed up and slipped up in the game in any way. Big Dez had what you needed when it comes to all-out warfare against The MOB or whoever, even the National Guard.

"What it is, bro?"

"I got some money fa ya. My people need yo help big time. Fool got that guop too."

"Big-time, huh! Where you know that boy from man, cause you know I ain't with that bullshit!"

"He good Big Bruh!" Capone assured. "You know I wouldn't bring no heat yo way. I been dealing with buddy for a minute. He got popped, and retaliation is a must. He just needs that re-up. You get me?"

Dez had doubt pausing for a second. "Yea, I gotcha... When we talkin?"

"Na!"

"Now?? Aight ok, check it out. Come to the Burger King on the corner from my house with him in thirty minutes. I need to meet, buddy. You know how I do!" Dez said.

"He Gucci, Bruh! I wouldn't tell you anything to get you mixed up!"

"Aight then. I'll see what he wants and do that."

"Bet that up," Capone said.

"Aye, C-P!"

"What's sup big bruh?"

"If this boy tries me, I'm gone put it in his life, Pone!"

"You trippin'! You'll see, the nigga straight. Trust me!"

"Aight, Bro. Call that boy and let him know we are ready."

Capone hung up and immediately hit C-Lo back.

"What's hood?" C-Lo answered.

"I talked to him. He ready na. Meet us at the BK on 30th and Busch in like twenty minutes."

"I'm decka."

"And, C-Lo just follow my lead. He doesn't know you, but as long as you show 'em the fetti, he gone bring you the promised land."

"I got the money, as long as he got the plan!" C-Lo said before hanging up.

When he shot to his bedroom, he locked the door behind him, moved his long green marble dresser to the side, and removed the wooden floor planks. 55-2-24 Pop! He put in his safe combo, pulled out his money counter, placed it to the side, and then pulled out the two Gucci bags full of money that Capone gave him.

After everything he needed to be led out between the bed and the nightstand, he started dropping wads of cash on the counter. Both bags added up to 105,000, exactly what he owed him. Meaning he'd bonded him out of jail out of his pocket. He put $50,000 in one of his Louie bags and dropped five bands in his pocket. By the time he looked at his Cartier watch, he noticed it had already been twenty minutes or so since he last talked to Capone. He threw everything he didn't need back in the hole, closed the flap to the safe, replaced the wood flooring and dresser back in its place. He then flew down the steps with a bag in hand, straight out the door grabbing his keys off the key hook without stopping. When he pulled off, he hit Capone.

"Hey!"

"Hey, what! Where you at, Lo?"

"I'm in motion! Ain't no pressure, fool! Everything A-1 on this end. I'll be pulling in, in about two to three minutes."

"Aight. We sitting here eating! Tighten up so we can make these moves."

"Aight, I'm decka in a sec!" C-Lo lived in the heart of Temple Terrace, so he was only five minutes away anyways.

When he pulled up at BK, he parked, went in, then ordered a bacon double cheeseburger with a sprite. He approached Capone and his brother sitting at a table located next to the bathroom. Capone was the first to speak.

"This my big bruh, Desmond. Dez this C-Lo."

"Just call me Dez. What it be like, C? You running kind of late ah?"

"Call me C-Lo, and you wanted me to bring some money, didn't you?"

Dez looked at his brother, and Capone instantly knew what his brother was thinking, "Let's get down to business. Lo, tell 'em what you need!"

"I need two-bullet proof vests. A few 9's, a tek9, a mini-14, and a AR-15."

"That's it you got 'em."

"Do you have a .45 desert eagle?"

"Yes. You need all that?"

"Yea, plus my people say they need a 3'5'7' a…"

"Hold up, hold up! I'm not dealing with yo homeboy, ya homeboy homeboys, or yo babymama and her peoples!"

"Check this out, man! I'm the nigga spitting out this cash! Ya dealing with me and only me, ya heard?"

"Yea-" Dez started.

"Well, fo' mo' then... just hear me bruh, cause I'm far from some window shopper fool, I got it, and I'm bout it. When it come ta that cash!"

After a moment of silence, Dez asked C-Lo, "That's it?"

"Yea. Oh. No! I also need a Glock 17."

"A Glock 17, you got nice taste. That's straight gunplay right there. You can go to war with them, Shh-, I got all that and some."

"Okay... Well, let's get this bit don then."

"Why you such in a rush. I was liking you for a second."

"Not to be rude, bruh, but you don't have to like m fool! Like this money! And my time is just that!"

"You right now! Ya damn sholl right!"

C-Lo followed them to Dez's house that was right around the corner. When they pulled up, Dez waved him into the garage. C-Lo grabbed the mini-sized Louie bag, following Capone and Dez through his crib, then exited through the back door into the guest house until they piled inside.

The inside looked to be just another old shed. The garage had racks filled with tools, hammers, saws, shovels, and all until Dez hit something in the corner. You would've thought the whole wall was some type of side elevator the way it slid open like in some movie. A sliding door led to a large room filled with guns, grenades, bazookas, automatics, gadgets, grenade launchers, and other warfare weapons on display.

"Talk about weapons of mass destruction! What's that?" C-Lo asked wide-eyed.

"That's the new fifty Cal Beretta from Pakistan. Only the best sniper rifle ever manufactured!"

"How much?"

"Twelve thou. You can give me ten tho! And it's brand new with instructions."

"Damn $10,000?"

"Yea, too much for ya blood?"

"Naw… Not really. Let me get it."

"Oh yeah! The twenty or the forty-round chip?"

"You ain't got no drums?"

"Not for that!"

"Okay, give me both then. Aye do you have an M-16, I believe the A-02?"

"No… I know what you talking bout, it's a beauty, but there's no need for that type M-16 if you getting the Beretta, the AR-15, and the mini 14, the 223. I also got some AK-47's with hail fire clips."

"I'll take two of those."

Dez was beginning to think C-Lo was just waiting, wasting his time, "Okay, what else?"

"A Tek-nine, an SKS, that 357- Mag, two nines…" C-Lo paused, "that Desert Eagle… I'm forgetting something. Ahhhhhh, oh yeah. Two bulletproof vests and extra clips to everything with a shit load of ammo!"

"You serious! You starting a mini-war for real ain't you?"

"I didn't start it."

"Okay, let's see." Dez grabbed his pad and calculator and reported the whole list. Then told C-Lo that he hoped he brought about 50,000 with him.

"I wouldn't have ordered it if I couldn't cash that check for the demands."

"I'm gonna throw in all the ammo you carry, with a case of high-tech knives."

"Bruh, I don't need no knives!"

"I'm just gone throw them in!"

"Okay, do that!!"

"I'm giving you a metal detector wand, a case of grenades...."

"You trying to get me ready to war against Iraq for real! Fuck it, I'll take it! All of it! What it come to?"

"$48,300... Plus, I'm throwing in a trench coat where you can hook this double gun holster inside, some camouflage clothes with bags. What do you think?"

"Man, how much you changed me for the fully automatic rifles?"

"$15,000 for all them never fired, still in cases."

C-Lo looked at him with a long drag, then toss the Louie beg on the dusty desk mocking dirt fly filling up the room with smoke. "Bet that up. Here you go!"

"How much you got there?"

"Just one." Dez paused, cutting himself off. How much you said there?"

"$50,000!"

"Yes, sir... Two Glock seventeens! I knew I liked you for some reason. You a man that knows what he wants!"

When C-Lo was packing his trucks down with boxes and bag after bag, he didn't notice an unmarked police car watching him from across the street, taking pictures of his every movement. When he left the hospital, he didn't know he picked up a tale he couldn't shake. Right now, wasn't a good time to get caught up with the boys, not when he was ready for war, with enough weaponry to bring down a small city.

Chapter 14

"ROAD TRIP"

The very next day... C-Lo and Gator took off down to Miami, Florida, for Cool's funeral. They went straight to Cool's sister's house, Mrs. Katherine, outside of town in Wynwood when they got there. They arrived there around 6:30 p.m., the night of the wake, the day before the burial.

"They call me stunna, a brand-new color fa hummer, Benz. I can ride everybody of the summer."

The house was packed. People were scattered throughout, chilling on the porch, hanging out in the front yard, pulling off leaving, and taking plates to their cars, getting ready to go. You could tell Cool was loved and had a big family and many friends. Gator popped his head out of his car; he had two twin girls with him, Brianna and Bridgett.

"Hey, Bri! Hey Briz!

They weren't little girls either. Both were five foot eight and between 140-150 pounds each. They have long legs with a dark caramel chocolate skin tone. Both have jet black hair that hangs down their back, almost to their nice juicy plump donks. You couldn't tell them apart. Bri had light green eyes with braids, and Bri had hazel green eyes like her mother with straight hair that unfolded down her back. That was the only way you could tell 'em apart.

Gator hugged them both at the same time, but the girls couldn't take their eyes off C-Lo. Finally, Gator said, "I'm sorry, ladies, this is my son-in-law, Charles." They didn't hear another word; upset hearing it was his son-in-law. "C-Lo, this is Bri, and this here is Briz. The Bri Twins!"

As he looked, the only thing he could think about was how beautiful they were. Their breasts were full, trying to find freedom. He studied their heart rose-shaped tattoos that continued in a view that read up Briz's right shoulder and arm: "Bri, sexy always-on". Up Bri's left shoulder and arm in the rose vein, it read: "-N forever sexy Bri". The tats were identical, like matching love lockets.

"Hey, C-Lo!" the twins sang in unison with the sexiest voices.

"Where's ya mother?"

"Inside!" the Bri twins said, sounding similar to Mary Mary, the R&B singers.

"Come on, Lo. Let us go inside," Gator said. C-Lo looked back at them as they headed towards the front door, contemplating the next time he was gone bump into them again; and he did mean bump.

Mrs. Cat stood at the front door talking to some ugly older guy with a face full of grays. She was forty-seven but looked damn good for her age. She didn't look a day over thirty. If she didn't have that straight, shiny silver dun-colored hair that runs down her shoulder blades, you wouldn't be able to guess otherwise. She stood five foot five with a dark smooth brown complexion. As they approached, you could see her thickness compacted, crammed in her jeans with her phat camel toe sitting up at attention.

"Hey, Boo! Come in!" she said. When she spoke, you could see three or four golds in her mouth. She had to be Jamaican with a spice of Brazilian favor. She also had a slight southern mix with an accent that was incredibly sexy. You could tell where the Bri Twins got their sex appeal from, their mother.

"Wow, I thought you wasn't gone pop up until tomorrow! Sit down! Want something to eat? Something to drink? I got some freshly made lemonade?"

"No, I'm fine, Cat," Gee said.

"Yes, something to drink sounds fine."

When she walked away to get C-Lo some lemonade, that's when you could see her jiggly plum forty-four-inch ass was just right. If you closed your eyes after seeing her, the only thing you could picture was straight pornographic material.

When she came back into the room, Gator said, "I'm so sorry. This is Charles, Tiffany's soon-to-be husband...and, C-Lo, this is my very close friend, Mrs. Katherine. She's like a sister of mine."

She licked her lips while she greeted C-Lo, "Nice to meet you, Mr. Charlie. You can just call me Cat." It had to be her sexiest voice. Any sexier, he might have nutted on himself as fine as she is.

"Nice to meet you to Ms. Cat. Just call me C-Lo.

The entire living room was red with see-thru plastic covering everything. As Katherine sat down, her legs opened up, and Gator's dick jumped like it was a silent beat only his meat could hear, and it was coming from her pussy cat. He fell into a trance, thinking about every position he used to hit her in when they were younger. "How you doing, Sugar?"

She appeared to be upset all of a sudden. "Gabriel, how you think I'm doin? I feel like crap! My brother was found dead, and I got to bury him with almost twenty holes in him!"

"I'm sorry, baby. It blew me away, too, when you told me the other day on the phone. Can you tell me anything about what he was doing, or what he was into and with who?"

Her face twisted up again before she found an answer. "Gabriel, I don't know, boo. I do know this much. He was hanging around some bad people."

"Bad people?"

"Yes, that's what the gossip on the street is."

"The only thing I saw was him throwing money around as if it grew on trees. I told him a week before he died that I had some bad feelings. I tried to say to him slow what he was doing, but all y'all always been hard-headed!"

"Where was he at the most?"

"He hung out at a lounge in Coco walk. All the time!"

"Coconut Grove off of Grand!!! Don't go down there!" She cut herself off and stared at Gator's dumb facial expression for a split second. "Okay, Go! See what's so damn funny about it then! I don't care to know! That's where they killed my Brother, Gee! So why go? He's dead! You gone get ya-self in some trouble or get hurt, Bae! I care too, but there's nothing that can bring him back!"

"I know. I just need to know for myself. I'm not just gone come down here and fall back. I need to know for me!!! I tell you what, I won't go if you don't want me to." Gator stood up. C-

Lo looked at him and rushed to finished his drink, then jumped up next to him. Mrs. Cat spoke, "Be careful, Boo. I already know you goin! You coming back here tonight? I have plenty of room for you and your friend." She bit down on her bottom lip like they were mouth-watering, then continued. "You both are very welcome! Y'all, not a problem here."

"No, we're fine, sugar. We are staying in a hotel up on 68th St."

"Nice to meet you, Mrs. Cat."

"Nice to meet you to Mr. Charlie!"

"Thanks for the drinks to Ma'am."

"No problem. Believe me, the pleasure is all mine... Tomorrow, Gabriel! Ten o'clock! Don't be late!" she yelled as they as they walked to the car.

C-Lo's mouth twisted into a smile. "Gabriel, huh? I thought ya real name was Gator the whole time I've known you!"

"Ya, a lot of people do. I don't like Gabriel. It's corny!"

"No, it ain't! It's a name of an Angel. That's a tight name. Gabriel!" He laughed as he waved his hands parallel like he was writing his name across Hollywood lights.

"See what I mean!"

"Noooo, Gee, I'm just laughing because of how you said it, and look at the way you looking! I'm just glad to know I got a Guardian Angel with me." They both continued to laugh while C-Lo was turned off his car alarm. They hopped in, heading towards the Legion's Lounge.

***

"Legion Lounge"

When they pulled up at Legion's Lounge, they couldn't wait to get inside based on how energetic outside was, but it wasn't any club or bar-type joint. It was a gamer's haven that also had movie theaters inside. It was very absurd to Gator because Cool didn't care to play any type of games. So not only did he think it was strange, he knew it had to be something special about this spot.

"Get caught with it, or don't let me see you with it, which I already did. Meaning take 'em back to your car, or you can always leave them here in my safe," Gee said, patting his other holster, which was empty.

Seconds later, some obese guy with Steve Nash jet black hair closed in on them. His nametag read: "Alex Legion".

"Duster!" Gator said in complete disbelief.

"Gee! That's you?" Alex tweeted back.

"Yes! This yo spot?"

"Come on! I've been had this joint up and going for almost two years now!"

"You said one day you was gone get something like this! I should have known this was ya scene, especially if Cool had something to do with it."

"You ain't seen nothing yet! What's the problem? Come on in!" Alex said, waving them in.

Eclipse looked down at him. "Sorry, sir, they had weapons on them."

"Oh, they alright, they like family! Come on, let me show y'all around!"

When C-Lo passed by Eclipse, he showed him up like he got lucky Duster arrived when he did, "Remember, with it or without it!"

Music was playing, but this was no ordinary music. It was more like strange devil-worshiping taunts mixed with Mortal Kombat sound bites. "Get over here!" "Flawless Victory!" "Finish Him!" "Fatality!" etc.... with a deep instrument, screams, and blood spatters... It looked pretty cool, though, with the black interior and different colored lights. Comfortable love seats and giant bean bags are scattered throughout.

Duster showed them around. There were big-screen TVs and flat screens sitting in multiple areas with X-box's, Wii's, PS3's. He even had computers and laptops, all with online play. Heading toward the back, you couldn't move around due to how crowded it was. He also had an area set up to bring your systems, such as Nintendo, Sega, Turbo-Gretx-16, old Atari, and any other old gaming system. Every set-up had nice smooth spinning chairs and paid all-day fees. It was a good investment for whoever was smart enough to invest in it.

As all three of them walked towards a sign that read: "Movie Station", Duster blazed out, "Man, that's fucked up what happened to Cool!" He went to open one of the office doors.

"What you mean?" Gator replied. "Who?"

"I don't know! I helped him do business, but I wasn't in his business like that!" Duster said. "Two days ago, after Cool died, the ATF tried to come to close me down. They had the FBI help and were saying Cool opened up my place with dirty money. I just opened back up today. They couldn't touch me or a damn thing I own! Bobby taught me how to jump rope around them crackers!" They stepped in the office door and he continued. "I knew somebody eventually would come by here to get the stuff he left."

Duster pointed at five big wood crate boxes, "There you go!"

C-Lo went over and opened one. "Floor tile!" The big wood crate box had oatmeal-colored floor tile inside.

"Well, that's what…"

Gator stopped Duster from mumbling, asking with confusion, "What I'm supposed to do with some big ass floor tile?"

Duster took a deep breath. "That's what it's supposed to look like. That's why the police overlooked it! It's really heroin!"

C-Lo and Gator's eyebrows raised in unison as they gazed at each other then back at the tile. They stood there without saying a word. They both knew what led to Cool's death instantly and what the Alphabet Boys were hunting. Heroin wasn't C-Lo's field, and drugs weren't Gator's field of expertise.

"We weren't ready for this Duster. Who else knows about this?"

"Nobody, as far as I know of."

"Is this a monthly shipment or a stash?"

"Stash, I guess. Look Cool helped me open up my dream place. I was and still am willing to do whatever for him! He was family!" Gator looked over at C-Lo, winked his eye, and told Duster, "Let me talk to my son real quick!"

Duster left and Gator locked the door behind him, then turned around. "What in God's green earth we gone do with all this heroin?"

"I don't know, Gee. It's like three to probably five million dollars here, if not mo! We not ready to take on all of this, not up the road. I mean, we canna!"

Gator went into a brainstorm.

"We need to move it, but who else gone pop up and claim this, or who's watching this place waiting for a nigga, or whoever to make a move on this shit?"

"You right. So, what you want to do?"

C-Lo had an idea. "Look ya hear me. Let's leave it here until after the funeral, and then we'll make a decision."

That following morning, they attended Cool's funeral. It was every type of car you could imagine there, like stars, big ballers, and all sorts of pretty women at every turn. It wasn't big, but it for damn sure wasn't small. You could tell he was a good man, and they loved him. After the burial service, Gator and C-Lo caught up with Mrs. Cat before getting into the family's limo.

"I'm sorry. I know it's been rough for ya. It's been hard for me as well," Gator said to Mrs. Cat.

"Thanks, Gabriel. You're an Angel."

"If you need anything, anything, Cat, just let me know."

"Thank you, Boo. I'm so rude; this is your nephew. Do you remember Lil Amillyon? Amillyon, this is your Uncle Gator and his son, Charles."

Gator looked at him in amazement. "Hey, son. Man, how you've grown since I last seen ya!"

"Hey Uncle Gator," Amillyon greeted.

"Call me Gee, son."

"Okay, Uncle Gee! I'm gone take care of her. I'm always by her side."

C-Lo gave Amillyon a brief observation. He had on a pair of baggie jeans, at a funeral at that, with a pair of old shoes on and a thin chain; it probably didn't run him more than $50, if it was real. You could tell by just looking at him that he wasn't in the game with his Uncle Cool.

"What's good?"

"Nothing! What's going on, Charles?" Amillyon said.

"Call me C-Lo."

"What going on, yardy?"

"Everything Gucci, but before we leave town, I need to get with ya," C-Lo said.

"Y'all bouncing when?"

"First thing in the morning."

"Why not run cross me now?"

"Aight, aye Gee! I'll be right back!"

"Okay, Lo!" Gator said, catching up on old times with Mrs. Cat.

"What it be, star?" Amillyon asked C-Lo.

"I want who you think killed ya Uncle Cool, and what type of business was he in?"

"I don't really know who put my Uncle down in the bloody dirt. But him getting tons in special shipments. I think, yardy, whoever ships his work, believe he ratted...snaked them out, cause after last shipment com' bloody ATF Boys closed down central ship dock. It's over! No getting back to the blood clogs. Why want to bout my Uncle, anyway?"

"Amillyon…" A shiver of cold bumps ran up C-Lo's body; he scanned his surroundings as he finished his sentence. "I might find out what happened to that last shipment." "Yea, the heroin?" Amillyon said.

C-Lo looked around again, but this time cuts the conversation short. "Check it. I'm gone call you when we get settled back in town."

"Bet up, Star!"

"Listen, though. I'm gonna share with you what was shared with me when I was young waiting in the game. That is, it's a dirty game, so I expected the unexpected! I'll call you in a few days."

"It's in my bloodline Yardy!"

"M-I-B"

C-Lo walked back over to Gator. As they walked back to his Benz, got in, and pulled off, he broke down the conversation he and Amillyon just had.

"Gee, let me ask you a question," C-Lo said, staring out of the window into space.

"Go head…blow."

"Do you ever feel somebody watching you sometimes?"

"Naw! Why you say that?"

"Cause, look at that black Lincoln with the five percent tint over there… I had seen it at Mrs. Katherine's when we first got in town, last night at Alex's place, and again today. I really noticed it when Amillyon started talking about the ATF and Feds."

"That Lincoln Mark VIII?"

"Yea, that one!" C-Lo said as he eased off.

"Gotta watch every move cuz them eyes be on ya, gotta drive real smooth cuz them pies be on ya! Just because we stack and ball outrageous, them alphabet boys got us under surveillance!"

C-Lo's little friends had been taking pictures of his every move. The truth was, the Men in Black, they now called them, had been in on the whole circle. They knew about Capone selling large amounts of coke, Desmond, his brother's gun imports and credit scam businesses, Bam-Bam's Lieutenant position in C-Lo's drug gang, and that the investigation led to his death, along with a string of murders surrounding them in the inner city. They knew about Phats and a bunch of their small-time D-boys that flocked around them both, him and C-Lo's BMClique.

The FBI and the ATF even knew about Santana and Rico's untouchables and were trying to find out more about them shipping crazy amounts of heroin and cocaine from Columbia. They were already trying to bring down Cool's enterprise before he died, but with everything they knew, they didn't understand what C-Lo had to do with them. Now that he had popped up at Cool's funeral, they knew he was connected somehow. He was smooth and more intelligent than what they thought. The ATF's code name for C-Lo was "The Ghost." They didn't know if he was a cold-blooded killer or just a wise businessman when it came to the dope game. They had an idea but were as good as lost. So, they stayed on his trail, waiting for him to make a wrong move.

C-Lo and Gator decided to leave that night. They hit Duster's, picked up he heroin, unbelievably without them boys' insight.

Chapter 15

"INDUSTRY"

Weeks passed since the Miami trip. C-Lo, Jit-Red, Chief, 5P, and Cancer had their show at One Twelve and had a ball. Their passion and ability to perform got better and better with every appearance. They were not only about to take Tampa or Florida by surprise but the whole rap industry itself.

It had only been three short weeks since C-Lo had been shot and charged with his firearm. Big Yoda Boy and Snapp had whipped up them thangs and ended up with over 160 plus bricks out of 100. Rex and Meatball got the whole caboodle together to establish the so-called infamous Carter apartments. C-Lo helped them set up in the large complex everybody knew by "The Reds". One way in, one way out! The BMClique set up two men on the roof and men along the ground. They had opened up a possible million-dollar spot, and C-Lo was supplying the whole operation.

***

"RIP Dawg(s)"

Now, it was time to go to court, and tomorrow was judgment day. C-Lo was at the house putting the other half of the bricks in his floor safe, all you could hear was Beenie Man's song with Sean Paul and Lady Saw chiming from his phone: *"I'm a gangsta fa life. Sex ya wife take ya life and everything nice! Gangsta paradise! Pow! Every time you see me come around, bossman."*

It's 5P and Cancer is on the other line. C-Lo hits his blue tooth and continues to stack the blocks like Legos in the safe.

"What's hood, Can?"

"Nothin, this 5P. What is it, Boss?"

"I'm fooling! I thought you were K. You using his phone?"

"Naw! This me Fam! 5P's on three-way."

"What's really hood?" C-Lo asked, holding in his suspicion from Cancer's response.

"Man… You sitting down, Boss?" Cancer asked with concern in his voice.

He had just jumped up at the exact time from finishing putting up that work but answered, "Yea, I'm sitting, but I'm bout to make some moves. Make it quick. What's poppin y'all?"

"Man, I hate to be the one to tell ya this, but…."

"But what?" C-Lo asked Cancer.

"Big E." Cancer paused.

C-Lo interrupted, "What about him?"

"He dead, Lo."

116

"WHAT!!! What you mean dead? We just seen him the night of the show!" C-Lo said, flopping on the foot of his bed.

"It's all over the front page of the Tampa Sentinel! Somebody shot and killed him on Nebraska, Columbus, and the gas station across from the Discount Auto Store! They shot him three times. He died at the scene, Lo. Then they flew his body back to Buffalo, New York this past weekend for his funeral, and the homeboy Dexter was with him," Cancer replied.

"Dex! You ain't talking 'bout Dexter?" C-Lo asked.

"The paper says Dexter Leeks."

"No man, No! Not D-Money Dawg!!!" C-Lo yelled as 5P jumped in.

"Yes, my opinion, dawg. The Sentinel says he stayed at Eric's Momma's house up there until the day of the funeral. He attended it, but then they never saw him again. My bad, Boss. I'm sorry, dawg. They found "D-Money three days later in an abandoned building, with eight or nine gunshot wounds."

C-Lo screamed, "What!!!"

"I can't believe you haven't seen it. It takes up the whole front page of the Sentinel with D's face. The banner-sized headline reads: "Tampa Native dies of what looks to be Mob related!""

"I'm sorry Cuzzo," Cancer said, bringing C-Lo eyes to fill with water.

C-Lo had known Dexter since they were in fifth and sixth grade. Their moms were even close; they were family. He was the first person he met in Tampa twenty-plus years ago. C-Lo didn't know until three or four months ago that Dexter even knew Big E. C-Lo was real close to E, and Dexter was his little big brother. C-Lo thought about his little brother Chief and wondered if he knew about their friend's death. He told Cancer and 5P he'd holla back at them later because he was about to hit up Chief. With his eyes still watery, he hung up and reminisced on how "E" used to come to scoop him on any given day just to go eat. Once, he had come in a hummer, and other occasions a brand-new Benz, Ford GTOs, Hondas, and even a Bentley. He even recalled him getting a Ferrari for his babymama; it was nice. E was too smooth, the type of person who walks in a place and owns it immediately without saying a word. The last time C-Lo saw him, he and his boys did their show the weekend after he returned from Miami and was up at Gyro's eating after with the crew. He had treated everybody to whatever they wanted and filled C-Lo, Jit-Red, Chief with colored diamonds that hung low and sparkled, showing something along the lines of, "I get money!"

Jit-Red's eyes stretched, and so did 5P's.

"Ain't that ya boy E, Boss?" five p said.

Yes, it was Big E shinning, standing tall like he was an NBA baller. On and off the court, a baller dressed down to impress wearing a pair of green alligator snake shoes. As the other man jumped out the passenger side Cancer said, "Damn! Do you know who is with him? That's the defensive linebacker for the Bucs!"

He towered over E and was every bit of three hundred and fifty pounds... Both of them swagged walked right through the door.

"What's good, Gyro?" Big E yelled over the noise in the restaurant, pointing at the Arab behind the counter.

"Hey, Bossman! I got you! No mushrooms, right"

"Yes, make it two!"

"Okay, Bossman! It'll be right up in a second!" the little Arab told E as they walked in smelling like a whole tree.

As they went to sit down, the line of seven or eight people that were constantly forming out the door trying to jam in, looked at them like who the FUCK did they think they were! Big E looked over at C-Lo with a smile and greeted him. "You see, my boy! Doing it big for ya peeps, huh!"

"Naw, this ain't big, not compared to you and how you do it!"

That was not even two whole weeks ago, but the last time he saw his road dawg. Even though he didn't get his work from him anymore, they were still good friends. He closed his eyes and said a prayer for both his fallen comrades. "Dex, I love ya, Bruh... Eric. B. McCloud, may your soul rest in peace." *"Damn, I miss my dawgs. Many nights on the highways, hustling hard get it our way."* He fired up the fattest hydro blunt he ever rolled up and smoked it to the dome, thinking real hard about his life. Where was it taking him, and what was it going to lead to? A lot of stuff was going right, but more stuff was going wrong.

The Men in Black that were watching him, he highly believed were the ATF Boyz. He had various horrific visions of Cj, Bam, and Cool getting popped; everybody was dropping like flies. He took a few deep breaths as he inhaled in the thick weed smoke and spoke to himself, "It's time to fall back. I got to open up a legit business." He had just realized the game only leads to death; ain't no winning.

Chapter 16

"JUDGMENT DAY"

C-Lo went to court the following morning for arraignment. His lawyer Ms. Kelly told him that the state was ready to go to trial and the only deal was thirty-six months prison time.

"I can try and get you papers. It'll be three or four years."

"Try, what you mean try?" C-Lo questioned.

"You have to realize, Charles. They got the gun out of your possession! Meaning, RED HANDED! So, what you want to do?" Ms. Kelly said.

"You the Lawyer! If I plead guilty, do you think they'll give me three years' papers?" "No! Are you listening to me! If you do that, they can give you up to fifteen years, that's without a deal! That's what they call an open plea, and best believe the Judge will openly give you up to the max! Do I really think he will give you fifteen? No, but something close! Today we take the deal or set it off for trial."

C-Lo eyes grew large as he spoke, "What! Set it off and go to trial, lose, then get 15 years? Is you crazy? And three years is not a deal! Look. Tell 'em I want to plead guilty, and I want papers."

"I don't advise you to do anything of the sort! You only have had one charge all your life. We can set it off. Stall them out and go from there."

"I was caught red-handed, you said it ya-self!"

Ms. Kelly gave him a real hard, insane look.

"Okay, okay, okay!" C-Lo said.

They enter the court and wait until they called his name. Not even 10 minutes flew by, and he got his wish.

"Next case! The State vs. Charles L Jones, case number 08-800551-0!"

"Present, Your Honor. My name is Sarah N. Kelly from Kelly and Kelly's Associates Law Firm. I represent the defendant, Charles L Jones, in this case. I want to plea not guilty or set this matter off to a later date so I can look further over my clients' case."

The salt and pepper bearded Judge asked, "Are there any objections from the state?"

A fat White Lady that represented the state spoke, "Your Honor! I have an old charge that just hit my desk where the defendant, Mr. Jones, never came to court. It looks to be from 1996. I don't know why there wasn't a warrant issued for his arrest, Sir."

Judge Perry looked over to his clerk. "Yes, your Honor, he has a pending case from 96, alright!"

Ms. Kelly cut her eyes across at C-Lo thru her wire glasses. Judge Perry squinted, observing him. "Mr. Jones, why haven't you took care of the old case?"

C-Lo answered quickly, "I'll didn't know it existed, Ya Honor! I was a juvenile when I caught that case, Sir. I turned eighteen in jail. They released me and told me that I would receive my court date in the mail. Five or six months after my release, I graduated from high school and then went to college. I thought they had dropped the charges, Ya Honor."

"Now, Mr. Jones, hear me out. It's up to you to find out your own court dates. It is not the jail's responsibility or your mother's responsibility! Yours! You are too old for that nonsense!"

"I was a juvenile then, Ya Honor!"

The State prosecutor lurched her way back in. "Your Honor, we want the record to show, we are willing to offer Mr. Jones three years mandatory for this new gun case and the old ninety-six case combined. However, after today, the state is taking the deal off the table because we feel we have a strong case against the defendant. The new case carries three to fifteen years max, and his old case carries thirty months to nine years max, but we are ready to proceed if we can't come to an agreement." As she persisted on, Ms. Kelly ruffled through her papers, trying to figure out if she could refile that 96 case; she really couldn't.

C-Lo looked at Tiffany. Ms. Kelly looked at him, and he told her, "Let me have a word with my wife first."

"Your Honor!" Ms. Kelly yelled, "I would like to request a short recess to consult with my client."

The Judge told them they should not go far and called for the next case on the docket. They all walked to the hallway where

Tiffany begged him not to take the three years. But, he knew what he was facing. He saw the situation. For that matter, she or anybody else wasn't going to do a lick of his time for him. He still told them he wasn't going to take it. Besides that major operation he'd just put together, you know, supplying the Reds, he just had too much work to put in the street and… fuck prison!

When they went back in the courtroom, C-Lo took a glance to his right and saw Det. Moore sitting next to his partner Det. Brown. They were off in the corner with two men who looked like special agents dressed in black suits. Why they were there, he didn't know.

As soon as someone called C-Lo's name, his brother Chief and his boy Jit-Red walked in wearing L.R.G SGT. It fits, making them appear as real SGTS and Generals in uniform. Judge Perry addressed the Bailiffs, C-Lo and the rest of the courtroom.

"Mr. Jones! Because of the warrant that I have to issue for your 96' case, I have to take you into custody with no bond!" The Bailiff grabbed C-Lo and began to put handcuffs on him.

"We will like to set a trial date, Your Honor, somewhere between the next two to three months. I'll be on vacation the rest of this April and most of May, Judge!" the prosecutor said.

Ms. Kelly quickly rejoined. "I object, Your Honor! We still have the right to take the deal if we want to, Sir!"

The Judge turned towards C-Lo full of frustration and said, "So what would you like to do, Mr. Jones? Do you want to take the deal the State is giving you, or plea not guilty and go to trial on both your cases?"

He took a moment muddling and couldn't breathe. He didn't know what to do but knew he didn't want to go to jail or catch more time than he had to. Chief and Jit-Red stared at him; defeat covered their eyes. Tiffany's face wasn't any different, with worry written all over it. When C-Lo glanced over at his lawyer, she shook her head up and down, slightly gesturing yes. It felt like forever, but finally, after another brittle breath, he settled. "Ya Honor, I would like to take the deal." Tiffany broke down and busted out in tears when they sentenced him to thirty-six months in F.S.P., Florida State Prison.

When Chief finished fingerprinting him, he put his four fingers under his chin and lifted his head, signaling, "Keep ya head up." C-Lo shook his head, acknowledging him. "Hold it down, Bro!" C-Lo said, never shedding a tear, as he was hauled off to the back holding cell until they transported him to the Hillsborough County jail. As he rode up the highway to Orient Road Jail, he looked out the window, "I can't believe this. I'm really going to prison."

When he got there, they booked him in, and he had in this mind already made up if a joker tried him, he was gonna earth him. *They got me mad. I'm knocking brothers on the back, in my cell kickin hell I know one day I'll be back.*

***

"Booking"

While in booking, he used the free phones before being forced to use collect calls. He blew it up; the first person he called was his mother. She told him he did what he did, so it was no crying now. "Just stay in your world, man, and do what you have to make it home safe." Mom dukes kept it gutter and always stayed real. He got it, honestly.

The only other person who picked up the phone was his girl.

"Hello!" he said.

"Baby! You alright?"

"What you think? I'm in jail! Classification informed me that I'd normally be in the county three to six weeks before shipping up the road. I can't believe this shit happened to me, of all people," he said, sounding defeated.

Tiffany began to weep. "I'm gonna miss you, Pookie." She paused. "I need to tell you..." She paused again.

With a bit of attitude in his voice, C-Lo asked, "You need to tell me what? Finish!" "I'm... I'm pregnant, C-Lo."

"What?" he asked dramatically, not expecting to hear that.

"What you mean pregnant? Why you didn't tell me that before I agreed to take all this damn time?"

"I just found out, baby! I was waiting on the perfect time to tell you!"

"Well, you sho picked a profound ass time aight!!! How far are you?"

"Bout a month."

"You could've told me."

"I was, baby, but all kinds of stuff started happening so fast."

His mind jumped into overdrive when that poured out her mouth. Was the baby his or Bam's baby? Now she was cutting out on him, cheating right under his nose, but he acted dumbfounded and kept his cool.

"My baby will be two before I even get out! I just wish you had told me sooner. I probably could have done something different."

She stopped his train of thought. "I'm just sorry, baby! I'm gonna let you know everything, every step, every word, every hair. He or she gonna know you every step of the way, I promise!"

"You sho doing a fine job up to now!" he muttered sarcastically. "Damn it, man. Look, I need you right now more than ever, babe."

"Charles Jones!" He'd been booked, assigned a dorm, and a female deputy was calling out names to transfer to their pods.

"You hear me! They calling me! I'm 'bout to go to the back! I want you to do some stuff for me, and I won't be able to make no mo' calls unless you tighten up."

"I gotcha, baby, whatever you want me to do!"

He knew bringing up that Sam-Bam situation now wasn't the best time. "Call Capone, Rex, Meatball, Jit, Cancer, and Chief, and tell them they need to get their phones right fa me to call."

"Charles Jones!" the female officer called again, making him the last to check in.

"Look, hit the bank if you got to and put a stack on my books so I can hear what I need. I'll call you back later! I gotta go! And Tiff?"

"What?"

"I love you. Put that bread on there!"

She said she loved him too and ended the call. When he got to his dorm, it had been close to fours before he finally laid on his assigned bed. He laid in his top bunk, focusing on the ceiling as he was dwelling on the multiple events that happened today—not believing the chain of events that took place.

***

"The Shadow"

I pulled up in my driveway. After I parked, I reached in the glove box to grab my extra clip pouch. Suddenly, I turned and grabbed my leather laptop bag out of the back seat. I jumped out of the car and tucked my Glock 17 in my waistband. I grabbed my laptop out of the driver's seat. As I walked around my car, I hit the car alarm with my crushed diamond keychain and proceeded to my front door. Before putting the key in the door, I heard a twig snap. A masked man yelled something I didn't understand. I reached for my Glock but was too late to react. The gunman fired off at least four or five shots, hitting me three times.

*I felt the horrible pain burn throughout my whole body as I dropped to the ground. Blood started pouring down my side from my hip. The shadow casted off the man from the street light as he stood over me, "Why won't you die motherfucker!" he asked, firing more shots, hitting me, this time in my shoulder and my chest. As I laid there coughing blood, I could hear Tiffany screaming as I woke up, still coughing…*soaked up from a heavy night sweat. His cellmate, an old white guy with a long full head of gray hair, asked him in the most southern voice he'd ever heard before, "Ya aight, boy?"

"Yea, I just was having a bad dream."

"Ha! Bad dream! I reckon it could have been a good one. Mo like a nightmare, I would say! You were screaming, please! No! No, don't shoot me again!"

"Yes, it's like I know who shot me, but it's crazy. I can only see a shadow," C-Lo said.

"Boy, you might not even know. You have to believe in God, son! Do you believe in God?" the wise old redneck said.

"Yea."

"There you go, pray ta God 'bout it. If you keep living, you'll keep dreaming and that shadow, ask God; he may bring it to the light."

C-Lo looked at him curiously, "How you so sure?"

"Boy, pray and just keep living. You'll see!" his cellmate answered.

C-Lo laid there picturing the entire world, not able to go back to sleep for hours. Right before he managed to, he prayed to himself, "God! If I knew what I know now, I would have done a lot of things differently. I wouldn't have done a lot of the things I did at all."

Chapter 17

"SO, WE MEET"

The next day, C-lo and about 40 other inmates were transferred from Orient Road to Falkenburg Road jail. By now, he was in his assigned dorm. He made his way to the basketball court, where a vast crowd watched a 3-on-3 game. Off to the side of the crowd, a white boy stood that he knew by Stud Jr., but his real name was Mitchell.

He was a giant redhead cracker standing 6'2 268 pounds, all muscle. He was supposed to go to the NFL, but in his last year of college, he messed up his whole career with a hefty cocaine charge, but managed to only land a three-year bid. He was now 26 years old. He reminded him of A.J. Hawk that played for Ohio and now for the Green Bay Packers with his gold fangs.

C-Lo had to front him a brick about a year back. Stud claimed he'd got knocked off with most of it but still walked the streets. So, people start talking, and the talk was he was talking. The better word for it was snitching, ratting, dropping dimes! Whatever the case was, he never paid him back and had disappeared off the face of the earth. Until now! Stud stood with his dunder-headed goons as C-Lo approached him.

"What's up, Mike?"

Stud turned around. The sense of fear had filled him, along with the expression of owing in his eyes as he saw who it was, then shot him a friendly smirk.

"Oh, look a here, if it isn't ba ba ba ba, Boss! The real Boss! Da Boss of all Bosses! What's up? To who do I owe his pleasure to, I mean?"

C-Lo was thirty-eight hot at how he was surprisingly showing him up.

"What you mean, what's up? You know what's up, cracker! You owe me twenty-five stacks, cracker! I'm 'bout to take my pay out your ass!"

"What?" Stud answered, acting as he didn't hear him.

"What, what? I don't know who you think I am or who you talking to, but you thought you was gone run, duck, and hide forever?"

"Oh, I wasn't running, and I sho don't hide, believe that!" Stud said.

"Fuck all that rappin!"

"Do what you do then!"

C-Lo looked at him, "Na, I'm bout that; I hope you don't think cause ya little homeboys out here, I won't bless ya ass! You just talking... I'm 'bout to tear you a new asshole." C-Lo kissed both his fist as he threw his set up and said, "I love me!"

"You better have my motherfuckin money... Don't get ta ducking and running, when they go gunnin about my motherfuckin money."

By the mean mugs on Stud's homies' faces, it wasn't going to be a fair fight. At that very moment, the rec door slung open. Out of nowhere, some tall willowy dark-skinned guy outside to the circle told Stud, "Ya gotta tighten me up first fuck ass snitch!" He swung on the pie-faced white boy, connecting right across his jawline as he stumbled into his friends, that turned out not to be his friends after all.

Slim, the man who hit him, set fear in the hearts of many. For some, they squared up, and Stud tried to rush him. Slim sidestepped, making him miss as they faced each other again. Stud looked concerned but acted as he didn't care how swift Slim was on his feet. After they both bounced up and down a few times, Slim finally swung but wildly missed. Stud capitalized, grabbing him, trying his hardest to flip him on his head. Slim held down, controlling his little weight, making it hard for him to do anything with him. Before you knew it, he came out of the bear hug, unfolding jabs and hooks quicker and quicker. He added a fury of uppercuts trying to Roy Jones him, and boy was he connecting. Everybody thoughts were mutually the same. The fight should have been leaning the other way because of Stud's size advantage, but by the outcome so far of the one-sided rumble, Slim appeared to be a professional street boxer of some sort.

Stud's eyes had started to close up at an alarming rate. Knots were beginning to form across his forehead, and by this time, Stud couldn't see anything. Stud messed up by continuously swinging but missed terribly with a right hook leaving the right side opened. He hit that man dead on his button, breaking his chin strap—pushing in the whole back of his bottom jaw, making his jawline dislocate from both his earlobes. Officers quickly poured out from the tiny door like roaches, spraying large, robust cans of mace. Stud and Slim were handcuffed and hauled off. C-Lo and Slim made eye contact briefly on the way out before being dragged out and to lockdown.

Thirty minutes or so later, the pod was off lockdown and back to standard. C-Lo asked almost every single person who the tall black slender dude that danced like Sugar Ray was, but nobody could tell him who the hell he was. He just wanted to know why he fought for him?

***

"The Plan"

Days went by, and he came up with a plan to get up the rest of Santana and Rico's pay. He had other plans but couldn't focus on them, at least until the mess blew over. He had already made Tiffany move to her sister's house in Oak Groove. The work he gave Capone, Rex, and the rest of the BMClique to move wasn't like he expected it. Since he wasn't there, he knew they would soon be getting work from somebody else, so he called Capone.

"Thanks for using team tec!" the female operator said after the charges were accepted, "Hello!"

"What's hood, Pone?"

"You, what's good, Bruh?"

"Nothin! You know I'm fucked up, right?"

"Yea, I heard what happened. That was some railroad type shit. Your girl called me. That's why I got my phone right."

"I know. It is what it is, doe fool."

"What's on ya mind?"

"You want to go to my store and pick up some more clothes?"

"You know it. Tell you the truth. I was kicking myself in the butt, wondering how you were gonna get some pants and some new kicks for my family reunion. I need you to work some magic. You feel me?"

"Okay, Okay... Check it out then. My brother Chief, and you already know Cancer, the tall nigga who is with me at the bar on the weekends, knows what the play is. I'm gone have them bring you what you need from the store. Seventeen the price on each pair." "Yea, I gotcha. I need ten pairs for the whole fam!"

"Okay, they gone hit cha. Look doe. I got a deal for the God. I'll drop each pair of jeans to 15, that's if you take over the reds for me!"

"Take over the reds?" Capone asked.

"Yea, until them boys get right over there."

"Aight."

"Look, ya hear me! This the play. Rex and Meatball taking over the everyday functions, just keep 'em working!"

"That straight with me!"

"Okay, it's official then. You'll be hearing from them."

"Aight, stay up. Superb!"

"Aight, superb fool!"

C-Lo didn't hesitate to call Chief. The phone rang and rung then he accepted the call as soon as he picked up.

"You have a collect call from...Boss...an inmate at a Florida Correctional Institution. To accept charges, please press one! Beep-..."

"What is do, big bruh?"

"I'm Gucci! It's hard, though, not being able to do what you want, from doing whatever you wanted. Having these crackers tell you when to get up, eat, sleep, shit, and where and how to walk. They treat us like kids, but you just have to stay humble. The only thing this is a grown man's daycare center you can't leave. I hate this price!"

"Do the time, don't let the time do you, bruh."

"Oh, I'm not sweating it. Not happening, and it damn show ain't the spot. I'm just trying to stay focus and keep working on my songs."

"Keep writing, don't stop and come out the pen like Pac!"

Chief paused! Thinking about his time, "Damn, three years bruh!"

"I'm Gucci doe, Chief. They say when you get up the road it's more stuff to do, so your time flies by quicker. Plus, the food is better."

"You stay thinking 'bout your stomach."

"A nigga always thinking 'bout food." They both laughed."

***

"The Truest Alive"

"Oh, yea Bruz. You heard the finishing touches to the last song on "Grinding Season?" "Which one?"

"That one song where we had that R&B dude Pee-Wee come in and drop that hook you wrote. It went like, 'Throw ya hands in the sky- ta the truest alive- Blazin blunts getting high- me and my niggas gon ride-yea-, I'm real- bout mine-, I be the realest alive- for my peoples, I'll die, cause I'm true ta this-, life'."

"Oh yea, that was *The Truest Alive*. That was the hook I wrote for Pee-Wee. What's his name...Bruce?"

"Yea, Bruce! Your verse came out clean:

(Da-Ghost). Be the truest alive, toss you a dutch (get high) mediate with this loaded nine.: Beam sound: Gon get money, gotta feed my gifts nig! Yea, I'm real bout mine. In court looking at life- (I'm fucked up!) Would you ride lie or act pussy and cry? You can pray ta the Father, but I can take you to the light-! FUCK that! Set-up shop, get money all night- (that's right)-...."

"Yea, that verse was aight!" C-Lo said to Chief.

"Hold up. Did you say aight! Is you crazy! Was you listening to what you were saying! Man, that verse hard!" C-Lo's verse picks back up:

"This paper so free so free so toss a "G" you'll see, ain't another like me! (ah,ah). This reality is not a dream. It's in my bloodstream, without a doubt. Take care, fam by all means (got to)."

"I just never knew nobody put together words or heard a nigga's double drop harder than yours." The verse continued:

"What's a drill, only know ta keep it trill, nig get it how I live, one of the truest alive (Boss Man)! Think it's all "G," cur ass nig, I'll let you feel this heat, (Load 'em up) Rise realization leave you vision ta blar (get 'em)! Yea what we cooking finna fill the streets, (eel) one in the chamber shooting six at you peeps, (Get 'em) da realest, a gangsta, that'll blow ya brains in the streets(eel)!"

Chief rumbled on. "Yea, that verse was tight. You be killing your ad libs. Your verse came out super clean."

135

"I'd like to hear that joint."

"Me too, Boss."

"I've been thinking, Chief, and it's no reason for y'all to suffer for me being in here. You know, by not being able to get in the studio and putting down and all."

"We good, Chuck! It would be nice doe, to get back in the lab and drop some tracks. Is Tiffany at the house?"

"Naw, she staying with her sister for a while, but I'll call her so you and K can meet up with her and get the keys."

"Thanks, Bruhs, that's just what a brother needs."

***

"The Plan Phase 2"

"Yea-, but I need your help, though."

"You have a minute left!" the lady interrupted them.

"What's that, Chuck?"

"I hate that Chuck shit, Bruh, but listen... I need you to do this important favor. I want you and KP to drop off some of the demos to Pone and whatever he needs from the store. I can't trust Tiff like that."

"Bruh, I'll do it, but...."

"Chief, I already know little Bruh how you feel bout it, but the bills don't ever stop. You gotta go get this money for me. Plus, you know him! So, you gone do it for me or what?"

"I don't know that nigga."

"Thanks! This what the lick read. Go to the house, grab change for twenty pairs and drop him ten shoes at fifteen apiece. You know where and tomorrow is when."

Chief had to let everything he said soak in, "Tomorrow?"

"Yea! Make sure you at least take 10 Nike's."

"Chow time! Go to your assigned bunk for lunch!" Officer Upshaw announced across the PA system.

"Listen! You hear me?"

"Yea!" Chief said.

"The combo to the safe is Momma birth year. My day of birth and the day Grandma passed away. 55/02/24... you and K can use the studio whenever y'all want to...be safe Bruh!"

"Aight, superb!"

"Superb fool... Oh yeah, Capone # is 813-225-26...."

"Thank you for using team tech! Goodbye!" the operator said, cutting off C-Lo from giving Chief Capone's cell. After he ate lunch, he hit Tiffany.

"Hey, Pookie!"

"Oh, you sound sick."

"I've been experiencing a lot of morning sickness lately, but besides that, I'm good. Sick of missing the hell out of you."

"Awww... when you gone see the doctor?"

"I have an appointment next week Thursday. He told me we gonna take a look at the baby, to make sure he or she growing right and healthy."

"Let me know what he says. Does he know if it's a boy or a girl yet?"

"Too early, I guess…."

After they talked for a while, C-Lo bust out and said, "I need you again, babe."

"Don't change the subject now, freak!"

"Naw Naw! I'm for real! I need you to call Chief so I can have you meet up with him to give him and Cancer studio keys."

"Okay. Today?"

"Yea, sometime today, don't forget to give him Capone number."

"You have a minute left," the lady operator said.

"Okay, baby. I told you whatever you need, I gotcha."

They said their love you and goodbyes before they hung up. She hopped right on exactly what her man told her to do and called Chief.

Chapter 18

"REUNION"

The next day, back on the turf, Dang was out shopping since he had stumbled upon some newfound cash, up on 22nd and Hillsborough in Tampa Fashion's Shopping Center. He stepped into the old ladies' bling-bling store and checked out an expensive chunk when he heard somebody yell his real name, so he turned towards the voice in shock. It turned out to be one of his old friends from back in the day named Bennie Thomason.

Bennie was 25 years old and grew up in Gainesville off 8th Ave with a clique of niggas like Deion, Wayne Perry, and Simmon Garden. Everybody called them Bad Lunatic Boyz, as he somehow graduated high school and he and his family moved to Tampa seven years ago. Most people called him Cal because he always carried a forty cal, but besides that, Calhoun was his middle name. Another reason was because The Lunatics went out one night and were forced to kill a dude. He killed one with his bare hands named Abraham, but his nickname was Abel for short. So, people grew to call him no other than Cain because he had 'murked' Adam and Eve's other son, just like that great story in the BIBLE.

He was a true jack boy at heart, a real gangsta with no remorse. Cain was the type that would shoot you and leave you in an alley in a heartbeat. He was of average height but worked out like the mad man that he was. His arms and chest were so muscular, steroids had to be in the mix. Half the time, he walked around with his shirt off or with a new wife beater on to show off how ripped he was.

"Naw!" If it isn't my motherfuckin dawg, Bennie Man! I haven't seen you in forever! What it's been like, five or six years?"

"Bout that."

"So, when you escape G?"

"I been jumped over a year now, boy."

"Damn, G! So, where you been at, folks?"

"Not holding up banks like you! I see ya doin ya thang boy! What you trying to do, rob this joint too?"

"Naw," Dang replied, cracking a smile, raising the bags in both his hands as they began to stroll away. "I'm just picking up a couple of things."

"Well, boy, it sho looks like it too, what a nigga gotta do, hit the lotto or something?" "Naw!" Dang said, laughing again. "I got a good job!"

"On Hoover Larry head!" Cain dared Dang to put it on the Boss. "I see it in your face, you lying boy. I already know you, folks! You sho can't stack 'em on the Boss!"

"Tell me how they feeding da God boy! A nigga gotta eat, fam. You already know I ain't on that 9-5 boy. Gone hustle from sunup to sundown and a click-clack a boy in the heartbeat if the price is right. Go-getter statics, by all means, boy!"

"You know I'm living like that, but by the looks of it, I'm in the wrong profession, boy. Real talk boy!"

Dang laughed so hard he started choking, "I can probably hook you up, folks! Lock me in."

They exchanged digits and agreed to hook up and go to the Zoo later that night to reminisce about old times and get back to the money. "Holla back boy!"

Around the same time that day, Tiffany met up with Chief and Cancer to give them the house and studio keys. Chief also got Cancer's cell number and called him to set up a time to meet later that evening at the Apollo and geared up to get back in the studio to work their magic.

***

"Apollo"

It was 9 o'clock already. The spot was super thick. Everybody and their mama were either there or heading to broke-ass Wednesday at the Apollo. Chief called Capone and let him know they were in motion. Before they all arrived, you wouldn't believe who showed up. Dang and Cain. It was a strange coincidence they so happen to drop off a pound of sticky to Rick for Phats.

Capone pulled up. As he jumped out his whip, he saw Dang outside buying a fish sandwich. They knew each other from Leto High School, Capone's only year there, and from bumping into each other around the way. They never messed with each other on that type of level, but were both D-Boys and they knew it.

Dang spoke, trying to make himself look larger than life, like he was balling out of control. If he would just let the truth be told, he couldn't get off the bricks he robbed Capone's partner Bam for, but we all know the white girl will eventually sell itself. He let him know he had that real deal when it came to fish scale as he lightly evaluated his fish sandwich, acknowledging Capone.

"What you working with then?"

They walk off to the side of the bar, they couldn't be seen from the main strip. Dang finished his sandwich as he looked around and surveyed his surroundings again. He handed Capone the yellowish-white brown block.

His eyebrows stood up awkwardly. What had caught his attention was the same brand C-Lo has on his work, and the seven squares he got from him the night he got popped was on the one he now held in his hands. He was stuck for a millisecond before he said, "I'll holla back at you cause my people's people been slow-motion lately with that work." Capone got his number but was confused on how he could've got it. C-Lo had told him the night he got shot, they didn't get any of the squares from him. Yes, he knew about his boy Bam getting killed, but getting robbed for some blocks didn't register to him. So, he definitely wouldn't know these could have been the same ones. Hell, for all he could have known, Dang and C-Lo could have been getting the work from the same person. That wouldn't have been that unusual if C-Lo wasn't cooking and re-stamping his work. It was very likely C-Lo's bricks resold with a higher price tag. His mind just wasn't ticking. Dang and Cain pulled off after, in the direction of the Zoo.

***

"Family Business"

Not even five minutes later, Chief pulled up in his new Malibu with Cancer. He had never been to Apollo, not to say the same for Cancer. They'd never messed with Capone, so they didn't know what he drove. To keep from going inside to take care of their business at hand, he called Capone, not even knowing he was there yet. Capone picked up the phone and told him he was already inside.

"Come on inside. I got us drinks and all!"

"Won't you just come outside?"

"Naw, that ain't gone happen! We don't do anything outside! It's better in than out. There might be eyes out there we can't see. Is this what y'all do? Come around to the other side of the bar. I'm sitting next to the Stripper's Entrance on the V.I.P stage. You can't miss me."

"I'm decka!"

Most of the BMClique and all the D-Boyz paid off the manager and the security staff to do their thing. So, it was never a problem serving or pushing weight at the bar. You know, as long as you were drinking. The Apollo was the most extensive dirty bar in Tampa, besides the interstate lounge. As they entered after a security pat-down, they saw strippers all over the place as he and Cancer came in. Dancer's coming out the stripper room, though curtains, swinging on poles, sitting at the bar playing bar games, pool, darts, and all. All types of booty was everywhere. They could hardly concentrate.

Chief came around the bar where Capone was posted up. Cancer stopped before and stood where he could see the front door and the rest of the bar. Capone sat on the private stage as Chief came up the stairs.

"You must be Kenny, right?" he said, blowing an immense cloud of weed smoke as he offered the blunt.

"Yea, it's Chief, buddy."

"My bad, Chief! Sit down, have a drink." He pointed to an Armadale bottle and a cup of cranberry with a bowl of ice by its side.

Chief sat a leather bag on the table and sat down next to him. When he opened it, he made sure Capone had a good look inside it as he retrieved the laptop. He sat the bag on the floor between them, right next to a matching leather bag. He then asked while he pulled the Swiss, "The demo 10, right?"

"What?" Capone asked, lost before he realized what he meant.

"Oh, yea, yea, yea! It's ten!"

Chief hit a few buttons on the computer and started burning a CD. He pulled the blunt again, then handed it over. He then reached and pour a shot of Armadale with a couple cubes of ice, no chaser. In the meantime, while inhaling that good green, Capone told himself, "C-Lo and his brother are two smart motherfuckers."

As Chief relaxed, he asked, "This piece always be jumping like this?"

"Yea, a lot of these niggas in here getting they pay up and some penny hustling. Me, I just be chilling dealing with the big boys while playing with these chicken heads!" As he said that, the CD popped out. Chief put the finished demo in a sleeve and handed it to him.

"Where's the ten dollars?" Chief joked.

Capone pointed at the ten-dollar bill he had in place already sitting on the table. They laughed as he closed up the laptop and reached down next to his feet to grab the matching bag to put the computer in. He sat it on the table and peeped inside it. After glancing inside, he zipped it up and slid the laptop into the side pocket. Chief stood, then downed a double shot of Armadale and cleared his throat, "If you need me, just hit me… It's a bunch of our jams off the album on that piece. Let me know what you think!" "Aight, I'll holla back," Capone said.

Before he left, he picked up the ten dollars, put it in his pocket and took the rest of the blunt offered and walked around the bar puffing on the blunt, giving Cancer a lite nod. He followed him out the door, but before they walked out, Chief dropped the ten-dollar bill in the tip jar on the bar, disappearing out the door in a cloud of weed smoke. Chief never felt the intensity, which was butterflies in his stomach. It might have been potent to the ten chickens he had in the leather bag he was carrying. He had with green before, but not powder, and not even close to that much.

Capone got the ten bricks, and everything went as planned. Chief and Cancer had adrenaline rushing through their veins. They went from ten keys of pure cocaine to almost two hundred dollars large on them. They fired up a blunt, doing the best thing they could at the time, and pulled off. They took the cash to C-Lo's house, dropped the loot in his spot, and got right back in the studio.

Chapter 19

"THE ZOO"

Dang and Cain pulled up at "The Zoo" club; the parking lot was filled, with no open parking spaces. That how they knew it was stupid thick. Dang had rolled up two dirties while Cain drove his Popsicle Orange 87 Chevy Monte Carlo LS. You could spot his car from a mile because of his Sunkist $3,000 paint job, with the orange mirror tints to match. That's what made it stick out as a crushed soda pop can. Plus, they said 24's wouldn't fit, but they lied.

They pulled up playing that song by Jeezy and Plies, and boy was it loud with an extended back seat customized box of ten's and two 15's concert E V's: *"The hardest thing in the lot that their mine!"*

Cain found a parking spot close to the front door off Nebraska and Twiggs. If you have ever been to The Zoo, you'll know why they call it "The Zoo." It was the wildest club in Tampa. They mobbed off in the spot and found a good table in the back next to two females. Moments later, they all decided to get some bottles. Cain told Dang he'd get the drinks because the bartenders was too busy running around trying to get

146

everyone situated. The bar was getting bull-rushed and busier by the second when Cain heard some girl call this dude standing near Cash. At the same time, he bumped against Cain moving him out the way, completely acting as he didn't see him. Cain was hot because he hadn't paid him any mind at all. He had to be the dumbest box of rocks, not knowing who he'd just pushed.

Cash was fairly tall and every bit of 205 pounds. The dirty red complexion, probably mixed with a Hispanic Descent. He dressed down in some nice Habari Gani wear, a long Cuban link with a thick, shiny diamond cross that was bouncing off his belly like he just didn't want it. Cain saw he had a Drak Skull tattoo. He knew he was a Blood, a Drak Boy from Sulpher Springs.

Cash managed to get the bartender's attention and ordered three bottles of Drama; a new vodka that ran twelve-hundred-fifteen hundred dollars a bottle. She pulled them out from a locked chilled case as he whipped a knot that had to be close to ten plus stacks. He didn't look like he had been drinking, but after paying for his drinks, he stepped on Cain's foot through the demented crowd, listening to the Lil Scrappy song playing.

"You don't want no problems, problems. You don't want no problems, problems. You don't want no problems, problems."

Cain became instant fish grease, knowing the dude had seen him, but he played it smooth because he knew them Draks were known in Tampa for their trigger play and flocked in packs of niggas living like that. He shook it off, ordered two bottles of Remy X, and headed back to his table, still kind of heated. He sat down the Remy Martin bottles with the cups and cokes. Dang looked at him with confusion.

"You forgot the ice G."

"My bad, Dawg! But this boy at the bar just pulled out what had to be over ten bands!" "Where that nigga at?"

"That joker in here somewhere! I'm 'bout to touch that boy in the bathroom or something! Real Talk!"

"You ain't got my own, hit my own licks!"

Dang laughed. "… Whatever you bullshitting! Go get the ice first, G, then see if you still want to get in that boy's chest. Just don't forget folks, we got these hoe's fool!"

Cain looked at the next table where two fine ladies waved at him, smiling.

"Aight, boy! I'll be right back!"

Heading back to the bar on the Ice, Cain spotted Cash again. "It's gone be hard to get buddy, how packed this place is," Cain said to himself as his victim step towards the front exit going outside. "He just copped three bottles so he couldn't be leaving. He must be going to his car to get something. Boy, I'm 'bout to lay this fool down."

He followed him right out the door, step for step. He watched as he turned left in the direction of the parking lot. When he passed the corner of the building, he turned into the lot. He went up two or three cars and over three cars to a big black and gold four-door GMC Yukon truck. Cash hit his alarm and walked to the passenger side, where it was the darkest.

Cain had already closed in on him and grabbed his blue soldier rag hanging out his back pocket. He paused, folding it around his lower face to his eyes as he continuously kept his head on a swivel. Right before Cash got a chance to open his passenger door, Cain clutched. "Tighten up, boy! It's a robbery now! Get on the ground! Gimme that wallet and hush yo mouf! Right now!!!"

He hit him across the head with his 45 mag, splitting the back of his head wide open with one hit as he crashed to the ground, crying, reaching for his head.

"Don't kill me, PLEASE! Please don't kill me! You can have whatever you want!"

"If you don't stop crying! Boy, give that up!"

"Here! Here! Here!" Cash reaches in his pockets, grabbing all his money, phone, and some hoe's number, and threw it towards him in fear of his life.

"I was talking 'bout that chain, Boy!" Without counting the money, which was seven-plus G's, he tucked it all in his pockets. "Where's the rest of it?"

Cash wasn't moving or speaking fast enough for Cain, so he jammed the barrel of the gun in his chest. "Aight! I'm 'bout to shoot yo ass!"

"In the glove compartment! I swear to God that's it! That's all I got! I swear!"

"Stop screaming and put ya hands down, Cuz. I ain't no motherfuckin police," Cain said, keeping the gun in his chest while he sat down up against the door. In the glove box, he found a brown bag. He grabbed it and saw it was full of money—$15,000 to be exact.

"Just got a whiff of that brown paper bag money"...

"Yeah, boy!" Cain hissed and cut it.

Out of Nowhere, a skinny object caught his eye. It turned out to be a part of a chrome ivory handle to a 32 clip with one in the chamber 45 Glock extended. He cuffed it along with a spare clip, then looked down at Cash without cracking a smile. "Yea, Boy! You's a baller, huh, Boy! Oh, yea! Get up. Get up nigga! What the fuck you was coming to the car for?"

"Some weed."

"Somewhat? Did you say some weed?"

"Yea."

"Well! Where's the weed boy?"

"Under the passenger seat. It's a secret drawer that pulls out."

Cain went straight to it and pulled out a pound bag that looked a little under a pound of crispy loose weed. "Yea, Boy! That's what I'm talking 'bout, Boy." He busted out with joy before turning to Cash. "You swore to God! You stood here and lied on God's name!"

"Don't kill me, please! I got kids!"

"Me too nigga! They thank you!" Cain replied, hitting him across his head, knocking him to the backseat, continuously hitting him until he was cold. Blood changed the interior color and was dripping off the door, seats, headrests, and lights all over the carpet.

He stuffed his legs in the truck while mumbling, "Boy, I know this isn't one of them same niggas hollering get it like Drak. Tuhh." Cain laughed, knocking him out cold again. He slammed the door and locked up the truck with the remote before he slung the keys so far, they wouldn't be found. He looked around, "On Boss, that was like takin candy from a baby."

"Put a cappin' to dat boy! What happened dat boy? Put a cappin' to dat boy! What happened dat boy?"

He cleaned the blood that covered his hand with his blue bandana as he walked back to the opposite side of the building where he'd parked Dang's car. He got to the marvelous Sunkist painted MC, popped the trunk, and dropped everything he'd just came upon in the back corner under an old Beast wear jacket. He grabbed a sandwich bag out of the large weed bag and went back into the club as nothing happened.

When he got inside and back to the table, the chicks were nowhere in sight. Dang sat there with one bottle and just threw up his hands in disappointment. "Where the fuck you been nigga? You still forgot the ice!"

"Damn! My bad, folks. On the Boss, I forgot, but I got something better than ice!"

He held up the seven-Gs, then tossed the half ounce of Crispy at him, "There was mo' then this where that came from, boy!"

They both smiled. All Dang could do was Chuckle at his homeboy.

"That's my Boy! That's my boy."

References

Lil Wayne, "Tha Block Is Hot"

50 Cent, "Get Rich or Die Tryin'"

2Pac, "Death Around the Corner"

Floetry, "Say Yes"

TLC, "Creep"

Jeezy, "Jeezy the Snowman"

Tony Toni Tone, "Anniversary"

Jodeci, "Feenin"

Juvenile, "She Get it From Her Mama"

R. Kelly, "Sex Me (Parts I & II)"

T.I., "Stand Up Guy"

2Pac, "Wonder Why They Call You Bitch"

Jeezy, "Trap Star (she Like It)"

50 Cent, "Many Men (Wish Death)"

Shawty Lo, "Dey Know"

2Pac, "No More Pain"

2pac, "Me and My Girlfriend"

Beenie Man, "Bossman"

Nappy Headz, "Robbery"

Young Jeezy, Juelz Santana, Lil Wayne, Fat Joe, Rick Ross & Dre-Dj Khaled, "Brown Paper Bag"

Birdman Ft. Clipse, "What Happened to That Boy"

About the Author

Charles Spraggins is an author, entrepreneur, musician, and producer from Tampa, Florida. As the CEO of Kingcago Entertainment Charles runs a recording entertainment company that helps artists develop and showcase their craft. Artists are encouraged to cultivate their talent and grow beyond the limits of the industry. By embracing the experiences throughout his life, Mr. Spraggins has gifted his audience with the new, insightful, and inspirational writing, If Knew, What I Know Now.

Spraggins N Spraggins LLC
2780 E. Fowler Ave Suite 409
Tampa FL 33612
(727) 488-4783

info@charlesspraggins.com

www.kingcagoentertainment.com

https://www.facebook.com/Charles-Spraggins-Author-104179018607365/

https://twitter.com/AuthorSpraggins

https://www.youtube.com/channel/UCdoQh2Eo-ieIemSmVcOm0Sg

https://www.instagram.com/charlesspraggins_author/

https://www.facebook.com/Charles-Spraggins-Author-104179018607365/